The
Angles Way

Walking in an Historic Landscape

Kate Skipper and Tom Williamson

First Published 1993
by the Centre of East Anglian Studies

ISBN 0-906219-34-5

Book design and front cover photograph
by Colin Blake

Printed in Great Britain by Crowes of Norwich

Contents

Foreword

I am not certain how many actual Angles roamed the area of the *Angles Way* - even experts like the authors of this book cannot, as it were, know all the Angles - but we do know they came to settle in East Anglia, and like so many of the incomers who have followed them, they liked what they saw. These days they would find it a lot easier to explore the border country between Norfolk and Suffolk, thanks to the linking of various tracks and footpaths to create the Way named after them; and with the help of these pages, they could not only enjoy walking through some of East Anglia's most delightful and typical countryside, they would also understand how it got that way.

This book could easily be sub-titled: "Everything You Ever Wanted to Know About the East Anglian Countryside, Plus A Lot You Thought You Knew Already", because its contents are not just confined to the Waveney and Little Ouse valley. It skilfully uses a feature of that area, perhaps a drainage pump or a round-towered church, as the basis for a much broader commentary, in these cases on East Anglian land drainage systems and early church architecture. It may cover a lot of daunting "ologies" in the process - geology, archaeology, hydrology, sociology - but it is always readable and understandable.

It incorporates local legend as well as scientific fact, and I was delighted to find in the passage about round towers, for example, that besides explaining the conventional arguments as to why they are round - either they were easier to defend, or corners were too difficult to build - the writers also quote my own favourite theory. This suggests that, in the days when the land level was much higher, the towers were actually wells, and

(Opposite)
The River Waveney near Beccles.

5

as the land subsided or was washed away, the round walls were exposed. The early builders just put a roof on top, added a nave and chancel, and there was their round-towered church...

I have to say that the authors of this book do not take the well theory too seriously. They lean towards the latest school of thought, which says round towers are round, merely because the people who built them thought they looked nicer that way. It seems so eminently logical that I think I'll buy that too.

You will gather, then, that there is ample material here for the general reader to enjoy, as much as the serious student - anyone, in fact, who has an interest in East Anglia in general, and the area between Breydon Water and Thetford in particular. As well as its comprehensive coverage, it still leaves some fascinating references to follow up. I must find out more, for instance, about Sir Robert Shafto Adair, the first and only Lord Waveney, "author of a patently crazy book about defending Britain from the menace of foreign invasion - and indigenous insurrection". Does the saying, "Go to Bungay and get a new bottom!" refer to boats, or chairs, or trousers - or even plastic surgery? What went into a local Waveney cheese called Bang which made it "so hard that pigs grunt at it, dogs bark at it, and none dare bite it"? And most intriguing of all, what lies behind the strange name to be found on the edge of Flixton Airfield, "Starknaked Farm"? Could it be a reminder of the original Angles Way?

Meanwhile I am sure you will enjoy reading this book as much as I have. And if you can combine it with walking along the Angles Way, you should enjoy it all the more.

John Timpson

6

Introduction

The *Angles Way* is a new long-distance footpath running through the heart of East Anglia. It has been developed as a collaborative venture by a number of public authorities in the region: Norfolk and Suffolk County Councils, the Waveney Valley Project, the Broads Authority, Waveney District Council, and the Countryside Commission. The local branches of the Ramblers' Association were actively involved in selecting its route, which runs through some of the finest scenery in the eastern counties.

This book is not simply a description of that route: it does not tell you to turn left at such-and-such a junction, or to go straight on at a particular stile. Instead, it provides a guide to the fascinating and often beautiful landscape through which the Angles Way passes: to the history and archaeology of its fields, settlements, churches and houses. The two County Councils provided the funds for the original research necessary for this work, which was carried out by the Centre of East Anglian Studies at the University of East Anglia.

We would like to thank the staff of Norfolk Record Office, and of the Lowestoft branch of the Suffolk Record Office, for all their assistance; David Dymond, for reading and commenting on a draft of the text; Liz Bellamy, for her help in copy-editing; Graham King and Gus Govett, for initiating and maintaining the project; the Suffolk Mills Group, for the diagram of Thelnetham mill on page 123; and Jon Finch, for providing the bulk of the photographs. We would also like to thank the Local Studies Library, Norwich for permission to reproduce the archive illustrations on pages 41, 52, 58, 80 and 126; and the Lowestoft branch of the Suffolk Record Office for those on pages 42, 45, 48 and 77.

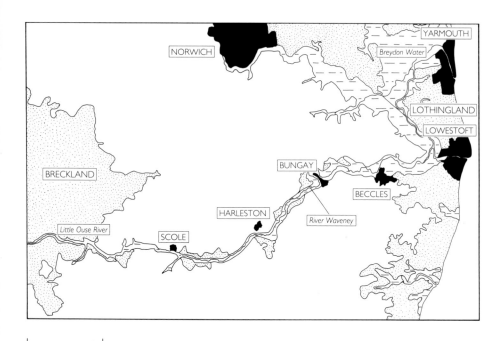

10 Kilometres

Drained marsh

Boulder clay

Light, well drained soil

I. Introducing the Angles Way

Unlike the Ridgeway or the Peddars Way, the Angles Way is not a prehistoric trackway or a Roman Road. A creation of the 1980s, it was formed by linking together public footpaths, bridleways, and roads with various stretches of new path. The name is a modern invention, but it harks back to an earlier period, referring to a group of people who settled in this area nearly a millennium and a half ago. According to the eighth-century historian Bede, the Angles, Saxons and Jutes migrated to England in the fifth century, after the collapse of the Roman Empire. Bede believed that East Anglia was settled by the Angles, who came from an area in Schleswig-Holstein, south of Denmark, known then - as now - as Angeln. This was no doubt true of some of the settlers, but in the confused folk-movements of this period, the original tribal groups had become very mixed, and people with other continental origins made their homes here as well. These new inhabitants did not come to an empty countryside. As we shall see, East Anglia was already an ordered and settled landscape of farms and hamlets, fields and woods.

In time, larger, more coherent political units developed from the confusion of the Anglo-Saxon settlement. A number of kingdoms emerged, including Mercia, Wessex, Kent, Northumbria - and East Anglia. The political centre of the East Anglian kingdom lay in the south of the region, on the coast near Ipswich, where there was a palace at Rendlesham, and where the great burial grounds at Sutton Hoo and Snape were located. The kingdom was of some importance in the seventh century, especially under its king Raedwald. But its fortunes waned thereafter. Dominated by and at times absorbed into its neighbours, in 869 it shared the fate of most of the English kingdoms: it was overrun by Viking armies. It was the reconquest by king Alfred and his successors of the Danish-settled territories, or 'Danelaw', which led to the unification of England.

Throughout its length the Way runs along, or close to, the valleys of the Little Ouse and the Waveney. Together, these form the boundary between the two ancient divisions of East Anglia, Norfolk and Suffolk: that is, the lands of the North Folk and the South Folk. In so doing, it passes through the very heart of the region, and through countryside which is typically East Anglian. Indeed, for most of the route, we could be nowhere else but East Anglia. A multitude of signs and clues, some obvious, some more subtle, make this clear at every turn.

First, there is the low relief, most noticeable to those who come from the hillier regions of northern or western England. Not that much of the countryside along the route is actually *flat* - with the notable exception of the great expanses of level green marshes in the area to the west of Yarmouth. But the relief is unquestionably muted, and the terrain lacks the dramatic incidents which greet the walker on the Pennine Way. The pleasure derived from the natural topography, from the slopes and gradients, is more subtle: and it is these same minor variations, in height and slope, which have influenced the development of settlement and agriculture over the centuries.

Secondly, the traveller will notice the prevailing patterns of agriculture. The valley floors of the Waveney and Little Ouse are covered by an almost continuous ribbon of meadow and drained marsh, but elsewhere almost all the land is under the plough. Over great tracts of the countryside, a cow, a sheep, or a pig is a rare sight. Wheat, barley, and sugar-beet dominate the scene, relieved by the occasional unearthly swathe of vivid yellow or ethereal blue, from the newer crops of oil-seed rape and linseed. It is a landscape of large farms, large machinery, and big fields, strangely empty for much of the year, but dramatic at other times, as in July, when the air reverberates with the sound of the huge combine harvesters lumbering around the fields. It was not always quite like this. In the seventeenth century, the great wheat and barley fields on the claylands around Beccles or Diss were

grassland, grazed by cattle. Dairy farms were common then, and local people produced a cheese called 'Bang'. It was a popular product then, but by the eighteenth century had become infamous for its strong flavour, hardness, and indigestibility:

> so hard that pigs grunt at it, dogs bark at it, and none dare bite it!

But over the last three centuries, East Anglia has become an increasingly arable region: something encouraged by the system of agricultural subsidies, the area's level terrain and, in particular, its low rainfall. And in the last few decades an even more pronounced change has taken place. With modern tractors and modern fertilisers, farmers have no need to keep animals to provide manure, or to pull ploughs. Horses, sheep, and cattle have all largely disappeared, and with them many of the hedges, ponds, and copses which characterise a landscape of mixed farming. They are irrelevant to a farming system in which the ideal productive landscape is a vast and featureless prairie, where great machines can be manoeuvred with a minimum of fuss.

An East Anglian prairie: view of a landscape devastated by intensive arable agriculture.

Indeed, in certain circles 'East Anglian Prairies' has become a stock term for the vandalism inflicted by modern agribusiness on the landscape of the eastern counties. People who have never visited Norfolk or Suffolk might be forgiven for believing that the countryside here has been entirely butchered, flayed bare

over the last thirty years. The reality, fortunately, is less straight-forward. There are some areas where vast fields of wheat or barley seem to stretch to the horizon: but in most places, hedges and trees are still prominent. And recent changes in attitudes, and in government policies, have led to a welcome upsurge in tree-planting. Little armies of plastic grow-tubes standing in inconvenient field corners, or in gappy hedges, are the most visible testimony to this. It is also important to stress that hedge removal is not solely a phenomenon of the last thirty years. Augustus Jessop, rector of Scarning in Norfolk in the 1870s, might have been writing the text for some modern documentary on the horrors of environmental destruction:

> The small fields that used to be so picturesque and wasteful... have gone or are going: the tall hedges, the high banks, the scrub or the bottoms where a fox or weasel might hope to find a night's lodging...all these things have vanished.

We are dealing, then, with a comparatively muted terrain and one predominantly devoted to arable farming. But this would be true of other parts of eastern England, of Cambridgeshire, Lincolnshire, or Essex. The distinctively East Anglian features are really the older details. One that immediately springs to mind is the incredible number of medieval churches. They are thicker on the ground in this part of East Anglia than perhaps anywhere else in England. Some are small, intimate: but others are vast and elaborate structures, seemingly out of all proportion to the size of their rural parishes. Many are stranded, curiously, in the middle of the fields, detached from the communities which they serve. They are flint-built, like those in the Home Counties, but they often have a feature rarely encountered elsewhere. Their towers are round, something which seems to enhance their detached, ancient appearance.

Then there are the other buildings of the countryside, most noticeably the windmills, scores of them, some in various states of ruination, a few restored to working order. As we shall see, many of those encountered along the route are not really mills at all, but drainage pumps, in the great marshes to the west of Yarmouth. There are also the distinctive features of the older farms and cottages. There is great diversity here. Some are brick, some flint, but most of the oldest have colour-washed plaster which hides the timber-framing within. Many are thatched, or else covered with the curious sinuous tiles known as 'pantiles'. The walker will come across some villages, where these houses cluster around a street or a green. But more noticeable is the way that in most parishes the dwellings are scattered in an apparently haphazard manner over the landscape, singly or in straggling hamlets.

These are some of the features which tell us that we are in the heart of East Anglia, rather than in Lincolnshire or Cambridgeshire. We can, if we like, just take them as we find them: note their existence, enjoy their distinctiveness, and leave it at that. But many who walk the Angles Way will want to know more. They will see these features as things which pose questions. Why are there so many churches, and why the round towers? Why do they so often stand alone, stranded in the fields? Why are the houses so often scattered across the landscape, rather than clustered together in neat villages? Why do so many houses have pantiled roofs? And there are questions to be asked about the most mundane features of the East Anglian landscape: about the age of a drainage ditch or a hedge, about the shape of a boundary, the antiquity of a lane or footpath, the purpose of a pond or a pit. We cannot explain everything which the Angles Way passes: but we hope to point out, and throw light on, some of the most interesting and distinctive features.

So far we have talked about the East Anglian landscape as if it were a single entity, with a range of definable characteristics. In fact, the Angles Way passes through several, quite different, kinds of landscape. The most significant variations we will encounter are related to the nature of the local soils, and these in turn are connected to aspects of the region's geology. The basic structure of this part of East Anglia is very simple. Everywhere, if we were to drill down far enough into the ground, we would find chalk. This familiar soft white rock was formed, more than 70 million years ago, by the accumulation of untold billions of dead organisms on the floor of an ancient sea. The beds of chalk - in places, more than 400 metres thick - are tilted, dipping towards the east. And so it is that, moving eastwards beyond a north-south line passing through the town of Diss, they lie buried with increasing depth beneath much more recent deposits, to which geologists give the name 'Crag'. Although, like the chalk, these originated on an ancient sea-bed, they are very different in nature, consisting of a complex mixture of shelly sands and pebbly gravels.

But this solid geology, of chalk and crag, is almost everywhere obscured by the more recent 'drift' geology, the superficial deposits which are largely the result of the successive glaciations which have affected the region over the last half million years or so. It is these clays, sands and gravels which give the East Anglian landscape most of its character and diversity. Ice sheets and glaciers, as they moved over the surface of the land, collected and transported a great deal of material. People may think of glaciers as something fresh and clean, like a glacier mint or an ice cube, but in reality they contain a mass of stones and rocks, carried within a matrix of softer material. When, at the end of a cold period, the ice fronts retreated, the transported material was deposited in a great mass which we know as *boulder clay*. This material occupies the greater, central part of the area through which the Angles Way passes. Indeed, it is the principal geological formation in East Anglia, running in a great curving belt from Hertfordshire, through Essex and Suffolk, and into Norfolk. It was left by the first glaciation to affect northern Europe, which ended around 400,000 years ago. It is worth looking at the stones in the soil beneath your feet in a ploughed field as you walk. Many are of relatively local origin, but some were brought by the moving ice from as far away as Scandinavia.

The soils formed from the boulder clays are poorly-draining and were, in early times, difficult to work. But they are also very fertile, and are equally good as grassland or arable. In the area through which the Angles Way runs the clay deposits form an extensive, low plateau, cut by the valleys of the Little Ouse and Waveney, and by the smaller tributary valleys leading into these. This is a landscape in which very minor variations of gradient have made great differences to the history of landuse and settlement. In particular, there is an important distinction between the more level and continuous areas of boulder clay; and those places where the plateau is more dissected and undulating. The latter areas were easier to farm with primitive technology, because here rainwater could be rapidly conducted off the fields by furrows and ditches. This was much less easy on the areas of level ground, and in the past these tended to be occupied by commons, greens, and woods.

After it was initially deposited by the retreating ice fronts, much of the boulder clay was reworked by floods and melt waters, and redeposited as sands and gravels. Other sandy and gravelly material was directly deposited by the glaciers themselves. The lighter material was subsequently moved again by high winds, in tundra or near-tundra conditions close to the ice fronts. There are small deposits of sands and gravels at a number of places within the Waveney valley, and sporadically elsewhere within the boulder clay region. But the most extensive and continuous areas lie on either side of the boulder clay zone, at either end of the path: to the east, in the district known as *Lothingland*, between Lowestoft and Yarmouth; and most dramatically to the west, in the area called *Breckland*.

Breckland is the more distinctive of these landscapes, although one which has been changed out of all recognition during the last seventy years. Here the glacial sands and gravels lie directly on the chalk. The soils are acid, the rainfall low, and the ground highly pervious. For millennia, this was an area of extensive heaths. During the eighteenth and nineteenth centuries, however, much of the area was converted to arable: and since the 1920s, it has been subjected to the attentions of the Forestry Commission, and extensive tracts are now occupied by vast, sombre plantations of Scots and Corsican pine.

So much for the general geology and topography of the area through which the path runs. But what of the river valley itself? Our use of the singular, 'valley', is not a mistake. There are two rivers, but, unquestionably, one valley. Somewhere around Lopham Fen both rivers rise, the Little Ouse flowing west, and the Waveney east; but the 'Waveney Valley' becomes the 'Little Ouse Valley' without the slightest break. This is rather unusual. But so too is the form of the valley - flat-bottomed, and remarkably broad for the size of the rivers it now contains.

Geographers and geologists have speculated much about these features. Most now agree that the present form of the valley is, like so much else, the consequence of glaciation. Two valleys probably existed before the last Ice Age. One, as today, contained a river running westwards towards the Fens: the other a river flowing eastwards to the north sea, probably taking a more direct route than it does today, making its outfall at Kessingland rather than - as now - at Great Yarmouth. The reason why, at this early date, the two valleys formed a near-continuous line is that both rivers followed a line of weakness in the underlying chalk. Then came the last glaciation, the Devensian, between 75,000 and 10,000 years ago. This created an ice sheet which was not so extensive as that which had laid down the boulder clays some 300,000 years before. Indeed, it only just penetrated into the northern and western fringes of East Anglia. A substantial ice sheet occupied much of what is now the Fenland, however, and a lobe of ice may have extended from here some way up the Little Ouse valley. As the climate warmed again, around 9,000 BC, water draining from this ice sheet could not escape freely into the North Sea because its path was blocked by the residual mass of ice. It was forced up the Little Ouse valley and, overtopping the higher ground between the two valleys, eroded it, and united them as one. The substantial outflow of meltwater and ice transformed the profile of the valley, giving it the wide, trough-like form which we see today.

The valley thus created did not originally contain the wide expanses of grassland which we see today. Instead it was occupied by areas of marsh and fen, which were only drained in historic times. This process was particularly difficult in the lower Waveney, where the river was tidal: but everywhere, the rivers had to be tidied and disciplined, and drainage ditches dug. In addition, in the upper reaches of the two valleys, in the area between Diss and Gasthorpe, there were several large lakes. Some people believe that these were formed in great holes left by the melting of vast blocks of ice which, carried by the melt-waters from the Fenland ice sheet, had become grounded here. These lakes have long gone, having gradually filled with silt and peat. But they continue to influence the landscape, because the areas they once occupied have always been particularly difficult to drain, compared with the adjacent sections of the valley floor. As we shall see, some are still occupied by undrained fens.

The long history of drainage work to reclaim the marshy valley floor of the Little Ouse and upper Waveney clearly wrought considerable changes in the landscape, but such alterations were minor compared with those taking place at the eastern end of the path, in the lower reaches of the Waveney. Here, after the final glaciation, the river no longer flowed directly into the sea at Kessingland. Blocked by changes in the coastline, it turned northwards, and joined a huge estuary, shared with other East Anglian rivers, most notably the Yare and the

Bure. The vast, flat, green grazing marshes which we now see here have been won from the tidal waters by human effort, at times helped, at times hindered, by natural changes in sea level. This landscape is therefore the result of radical human intervention, but as such is an extreme rather than an exceptional example of the processes that have shaped the countryside. Everywhere, on the Breckland sands as much as on the boulder clays, the natural environment has been drastically altered by the activities of its human inhabitants. Left to itself, all the higher ground through which the Way runs would be covered in dense woodland. Over an immense period of time, this natural vegetation has gradually been cleared, and a new landscape created. The countryside we see today is entirely man-made, and the soils, topography, and drainage are only important insofar as they provided opportunities, or presented limitations, to man.

At Hoxne, in the valley of the Waveney some three miles east of Diss and close to the line of the Angles Way, there is one of the most famous archaeological sites in England. Here, in 1797, John Frere of Roydon Hall noticed, in the bottom of a clay pit, large numbers of flint tools, of the kind now known as hand-axes. So many were being dug out by the workmen that they were being used to fill ruts in the adjacent roads. He was the first person to suggest that they were of extreme antiquity rather than - as was then generally thought - the creation of the tribes who had occupied Britain at the time of the Roman Conquest. He wrote in a now-famous letter to the journal *Archaeologia:*

> They are, I think, evidently weapons of war, fabricated and used by a people who had not the use of metals. They lay in great numbers at the depth of about twelve feet, in a stratified soil which was dug into for the purpose of raising clay for bricks.
>
> The situation in which these weapons were found may tempt us to refer them to a very remote period indeed, even beyond that of the present world.

We now know more about this site, through a number of subsequent investigations. There were two separate phases of activity here, probably during the Wolstonian glaciation, around 200,000 years ago. These are represented by collections of animal bones and by large numbers of elegant hand-axes made of good-quality black flint, together with a variety of simpler flakes - less elegant but no doubt highly practical tools. These were left by groups of hunters camped beside the predecessor of the river Waveney. Careful examination of the tools showed that they had been used for cutting up animal carcasses, stripping and cutting hides, and gathering plant foods. Analysis of the animal bones revealed that horse was the principal animal hunted here, together with deer, bison - and *elephant*, an animal it is hard to imagine roaming around the present Suffolk landscape. Tools of similar or greater antiquity have been found at a number of other sites in the valley, and in Breckland and Lothingland. During much of the 400,000 years which preceded the end of the last glaciation, especially during the warmer periods, large parts of the area may have been exploited by small bands of hunters.

Such activities continued after the end of the final glaciation, around 10,000 years ago, during the period which archaeologists conventionally refer to as the Mesolithic. But none of these early hunters left any features in the landscape which are still visible today. Indeed, they probably made little impact on the environment at all. Only with the advent of farming in the region, in the Neolithic period (c.4500 - 2300 BC) did the first significant clearances of the woodland occur. Even these inroads into the wilderness were of a relatively minor nature, and limited to the lighter soils, especially in Breckland. Within the boulder clay area, settlement was probably restricted to the valleys of the Little Ouse and the Waveney.

One important site from this period lies close to the line of the Way, at Broome Heath in the Waveney valley. Here there is a *long barrow*, a trapezoid-shaped mound which is slightly higher at its north-eastern end, and flanked by ditches. This has not been excavated in recent times but was presumably, like others elsewhere in England, raised over a timber chamber containing a group of burials. It was probably more than just a burial place, having a more general religious significance, as the ceremonial focus for a small group of related farming families. This monument did not stand in isolation: it partly overlies a contemporary or near-contemporary settlement, which may have extended over several hectares.

At a rather later date, a short distance away, a C-shaped earthwork enclosure was built, defined by two closely-spaced banks. The larger, inner bank had an external timber revetment and, perhaps, a palisade. A four-posted feature - possibly a small tower of some kind - stood at one end. But these banks cannot have been intended as a defence, as the enclosure was completely open on its eastern side. Like the barrow, and like many features of the Neolithic landscape, it was probably a religious, ceremonial feature.

It was not until the end of the third millennium BC, in the early Bronze Age, that farming and settlement began to make a significant impact on the environment. In Breckland, mixed farming became widespread on the more chalky soils, and even the higher more acid areas began to be opened up and used for grazing. Clearance extended in Lothingland, and it is likely that settlement intensified on the better drained soils of the Waveney valley. The most common upstanding monument from this period is the *round barrow*, a number of which exist in or beside the valley, or did so until recently. These were usually raised over a single initial or 'primary' burial, although further 'secondary' burials might be inserted into the mound at a later date. A number were built beside the Broome Heath Long Barrow, showing the way in which certain places continued to be of religious importance for many hundreds of years. A good example of a round barrow can be seen near the western termination of the Angles Way, on Knettishall heath.

But while settlement might have intensified on the lighter soils in the Bronze Age it was only in the last centuries of the prehistoric period, during the later Iron Age, that it began to expand on to the boulder clays. The evidence for this comes from field walking, the technique of systematically examining the surface of the ploughsoil to find concentrations of pottery sherds or other debris indicating the sites of early settlements. Field walking surveys suggest that one or two Iron Age settlements can be found in every parish, even on the heaviest clays. Supporting evidence has come from an analysis made of pollen collected from deposits on the floor of Diss Mere, a small lake which lies in the heart of the boulder clay region. In waterlogged conditions, pollen grains can survive indefinitely, and are able to provide a picture of the vegetation of the surrounding area at various times in the past. Work carried out at the Mere shows that until the last century or two before the Roman invasion, most of the clay plateau was covered in woodland. But it was then rapidly cleared. By the start of the Roman period, there was probably little woodland left in the area, and settlement intensified. Field walking surveys indicate that there were two or three Roman sites in most parishes, generally small farms and hamlets, but with some larger settlements. By the third century AD the entire length of the Way, from Lothingland to Breckland, would have passed through settled farmland, interspersed with areas of woodland and rough grazing. A countryside had been carved from a wilderness.

At first sight this expansion of population and farmland in late prehistoric and Roman times appears to have left little mark on the landscape, with the obvious, and dramatic, exception of the great Roman fort of Burgh Castle, built where the river Waveney flowed out into its huge estuary. But as we shall see, it is likely that some, perhaps many, of the lanes, paths and field boundaries which run across the boulder clay plateau originated in this remote period.

In late Roman times, for reasons which are not clearly understood, the population - here, as throughout England - appears to have fallen. The Angles, when they began to settle here in the fifth century, came to a country whose native population was declining. Farms and hamlets retreated from the heavier clays, and settlement became concentrated once again on the lighter soils. There may have been some regeneration of woodland although not - to judge from the evidence from Diss Mere - on a very large scale. This retrenchment of settlement onto better-drained land may have been associated with a change in the climate, involving an increase in rainfall, which made the clay soils more difficult to farm. Certainly, there is little evidence that land was abandoned on the poorer, but much more freely-draining, soils of Breckland. Here large numbers of early Anglian cemeteries have been discovered, together with a number of settlements, like that which has been partly reconstructed at West Stow, near Bury St Edmunds.

Settlement expanded onto the clays once more during the later centuries of the Saxon period. By the time of the Norman Conquest, to judge from the information given in Domesday Book, these were much more densely settled than the lighter soils of Breckland or Lothingland. Indeed, they were among the most populous and most intensively farmed areas in the whole of England. These fertile soils continued to be crowded and wealthy throughout the Middle Ages, and by the thirteenth century they were almost entirely under the plough. The only exceptions were areas of common land, which occupied the more level and poorly-draining areas of the plateau, and the floors of some of the larger valleys. These open areas, although notionally owned by manorial lords, were used as of right by members of the local communities, mainly for grazing but also as a source of fuel.

The ever-expanding arable land took the form of *open-fields*. The land of each farm lay in a number of very small strips, which were intermixed with those of other farmers and subject to some measure of communal regulation. But East Anglian open fields were not quite like those in the Midlands, which appear in all the school text-books. They were 'irregular' field systems, to use the jargon of the historical geographers, which were less rigidly communal in their organisation. In the Midlands, the strips of each holding were scattered evenly throughout the lands of each village. But in East Anglia they tended to be more clustered, in the vicinity of the farmstead. The strips in Midland villages, moreover, were organised into two or three great 'fields', one of which lay fallow each year, so that a third or a half of each parish, in a huge continuous block, could be grazed in common by the village herds and flocks. East Anglian field systems had a looser, more flexible arrangement, in which there were often several 'fields' and in which the fallow land did not usually lie in a single block.

On the lighter soils of Breckland and Lothingland, population densities were lower. Here, too, most of the arable land lay in such 'irregular' open fields. But areas of permanent common grazing were more extensive, with wide areas of heathland on the poorest soils. Sheep were grazed here, and folded at night on the arable land - thus creating a permanent flow of nutrients onto these rather marginal soils. By the thirteenth century, some parts of the heathland were being used by manorial lords in a rather special way: as rabbit warrens, producing both meat and fur. A warren was established at Brandon by 1251, and by the fourteenth century they were widespread.

By 1300 East Anglia, like most other areas of lowland England, was over-populated relative to its resources and technology. But things then changed rapidly. Climatic deterioration, poor harvests, and animal epidemics were followed in 1348/9 by the terrible Black Death, which reduced the population, within a short space of time, by as much as a third. There were fewer people, but the local economy continued, for the most part, to flourish, becoming more sophisticated and more specialised. Larger, more competitive holdings were created by the local gentry, and by yeomen farmers.

On the claylands, especially on the more level parts of the plateau, landowners began to enclose their open-field land, and put much of it down to grass. In the sixteenth and seventeenth centuries this became a dairying area, although arable crops were also extensively grown. On these fertile soils small farmers did well at this time, and a variety of cottage industries, especially those related to the manufacture of linen cloth, flourished. This was a landscape dominated by the prosperous farmer and the minor squire, rather than a land of great estates. On the lighter soils of Breckland and Lothingland, however, things were rather different. These areas continued to specialise in arable crops and sheep - they were areas of 'sheep-corn husbandry'- although rabbit warrens were also important. Large-scale arable production tended to be most profitable on large farms, and these areas saw a gradual decline in the number of small landowners, and the consolidation of land in the hands of large estates. These developments were accompanied by the shrinkage, or abandonment, of many villages. In the eighteenth and nineteenth centuries large amounts of money were invested in schemes of land improvement. With the widespread adoption of new farming practices, involving the cultivation of turnips and improved grasses, the elimination of fallows, and the improvement of the more acid land by marling, the heaths and open fields were enclosed, and warrens destroyed. These areas came to be dominated by great landed estates, and the landscape still reflects this in a multitude of ways.

This important distinction, between the claylands and the lighter soils, continues to influence the development of the landscape, with much of the lighter land, particularly in Breckland, now planted with conifer plantations, and the heavier land given over almost exclusively to great arable fields. But although these differences are ultimately related to soils and geology, their immediate causes are the variations in the way successive societies have exploited the possibilities presented by nature.

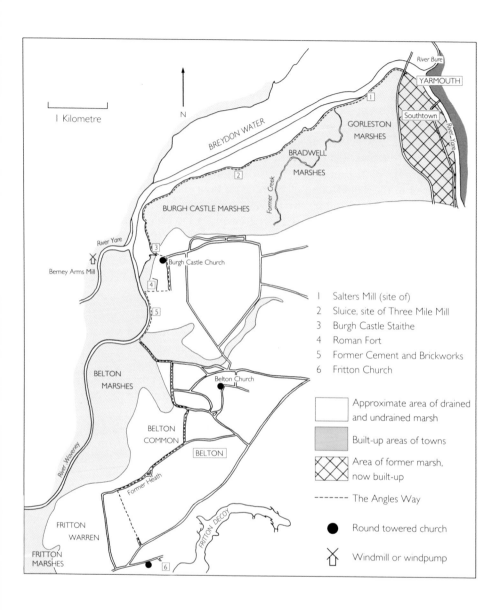

1 Kilometre

N

River Bure

YARMOUTH

Southtown

GORLESTON
MARSHES

BREYDON WATER

BRADWELL

MARSHES

Former Creek

BURGH CASTLE MARSHES

River Yare

Berney Arms Mill

Burgh Castle Church

BELTON
MARSHES

Belton Church

BELTON
COMMON

BELTON

River Waveney

Former Heath

FRITTON
WARREN

FRITTON DECOY

FRITTON
MARSHES

1 Salters Mill (site of)
2 Sluice, site of Three Mile Mill
3 Burgh Castle Staithe
4 Roman Fort
5 Former Cement and Brickworks
6 Fritton Church

Approximate area of drained
and undrained marsh

Built-up areas of towns

Area of former marsh,
now built-up

------- The Angles Way

● Round towered church

Windmill or windpump

2. Breydon Water, the Marshes, and Lothingland

The Angles Way begins by following, for some five kilometres, the flood wall which runs along the southern side of Breydon Water. Breydon is one of the finest sights in East Anglia: a vast tidal lake, whose mud flats at low tide provide an abundant food supply for flocks of migrant wildfowl. It is a mecca for bird-watchers, for it is often visited by rare species, including an internationally important flock of Bewick's swans. And here, too, the walker with an interest in the past has a rare opportunity to look out over the broad, flat marshland of today, and visualise the very different landscape of one and a half millennia ago. For standing on Breydon wall it is not hard to imagine a time when, instead of green grazing marshes, a great open estuary extended at high tide in all directions, fed by the waters of the rivers Bure, Waveney, and Yare. To the east, where the large town of Great Yarmouth stands today, the estuary mouth was over five kilometres wide. All the surrounding marsh was tidal water as far as the modern settlements which you can dimly see in the distance on the margins of the higher ground. These mark the line of the ancient shore: Caister-on-sea and Runham to the north, Halvergate and Reedham to the west, and Burgh Castle and Gorleston to the south. This is the scene the Romans saw when they built their fort at Caister - a kilometre south of the great water tower that dominates the modern skyline to the north; and their fort of *Gariannonum* - which lies beside the Angles Way, to the south-west, behind Burgh Castle church. Breydon

Water may be an impressive sight today, but it is a minor relic of this immense natural feature.

Following the end of Roman rule, a great bank of sand built up across the mouth of the estuary. It was on this that, during the early middle ages, the town of Yarmouth began its life, as a small fishing settlement. The formation of this bank restricted the range of tides, and encouraged the build-up of silt and the development of a great area of salt marsh in what had been the open waters of the estuary.

Breydon Water appears to have been cut off from the sea by the time of the Danish settlement in the ninth century, since the name Breydon derives from an old Scandinavian word which means 'broadening', suggesting that Danish settlers perceived a widening in the river rather than an estuary opening directly into the sea. By the eleventh century the land within the former estuary was dry enough to have been divided amongst the neighbouring parishes. Indeed, its economic importance is dramatically indicated by the fact that some pieces belonged, as detached portions, to parishes located several kilometres away. Large flocks of sheep are recorded in the Domesday survey of 1086 in those manors which had shares in the marsh. The largest flocks were held by settlements on the northern and western margins of the marsh, but the lord of Gorleston, for example, owned 300 sheep and the lord of Burgh Castle 160. These animals, along with those of the peasant farmers, were presumably grazed on the marsh only during the drier summer months, as they were to be in the centuries that followed.

Salt was essential in this period to preserve meat, and many of the marsh-edge parishes had salt pans in which to evaporate seawater, at the time of the Domesday survey. The possible site of one of these has been suggested near Ashtree Farm, on the Bure just north of Breydon Water, where evidence of eleventh-century occupation has been found. Burgh Castle had three salt pans in 1086, which must have been situated beside Breydon Water.

The earliest documentary evidence for the ditching and embanking of these wetlands comes from the thirteenth and fourteenth centuries, although it is not clear whether this involved the taking in of new land, or whether the work was being carried out in an attempt to keep flood waters out of areas already being used for grazing. Perhaps the latter, for in this period the sea level was continually rising, and climatic change led to more frequent storms, which caused periodic surges in water levels. When flood banks were first built the natural creeks within the embanked areas would have provided a ready-made system of main drains. From these, the water would have flowed through the flood wall and out into the rivers at low tide by means of a simple 'flap sluice', the flap being held closed by the weight of water when the tide was high. A modern version of a flap sluice can be seen at the outlet which leads from the only modern pumphouse standing on this side of Breydon Water.

The natural gulleys and creeks of the old salt marsh were thus fossilised as drains and many are clearly visible, winding away from the flood wall, all along this section of the Angles Way. Later, the system of drainage became more complicated. 'Land spring dykes' were dug, to channel the water draining off the higher ground surrounding the marshes directly into the rivers. Lateral dykes, called 'borrow dykes', were added to increase the amount of water that could be stored between tides without flooding. One example runs immediately beside the flood wall. In some areas, as in the Halvergate marshes to the north of Breydon Water, embanked 'washlands' were also created, to hold larger volumes of flood water during the winter, but from which marsh hay could still be harvested in summer. And so, in addition to the meandering watercourses derived from the natural creeks of the salt marsh, a number of more direct drains was created. Little by little, over the centuries, the complex network of intersecting dykes and ditches was built up.

As drainage became more complex, as the sea level rose still further, and as the level of the drained land sank due to subsidence and compaction, gravity outlets were no longer enough and pumps were needed to take the water off the marshes. Some horse pumps were used but, perhaps from as early as the seventeenth century, wind pumping was the normal method. The earliest pumps were probably simple trestle structures, like that which exists at Herringfleet, preserved in working condition two kilometres from the Angles Way. But most of the windpumps which exist on the marshes today take the form of brick-built towers. They are mostly nineteenth century, although a few go back to the late eighteenth century, like that at Oby, which is dated by an inscription to 1793. Windpumps were much simpler in design than the cornmills which we shall encounter later. The sails turned an axle which was geared to a long vertical shaft, running down the centre of the tower. At the bottom this was geared to a large scoopwheel, located within the body of the mill, which worked like the wheel of a water mill in reverse, scooping the water up from a channel in the marsh and lifting it over the flood wall and into the river.

Three wind pumps once stood beside this section of the Angles Way, although no trace of them now remains. The site of Woolsey Mill has been obliterated by the development of Southtown in Great Yarmouth, where the Angles Way begins; Salters Mill stood near where the channel running through Breydon meets the Wall; and the third, Three Mile Mill, has been replaced by the present pump house. Across the water, however, the remains of several wind pumps can clearly be seen. As the path turns the angle between Breydon Water and Burgh Flats, the great black tower of Berney Arms Mill dominates the view. This seven-storey mill, the highest in the Broads, stopped work in 1949 but has since been fully restored to working order, and is open to the public. Apart from its great height Berney Arms might appear, at first sight, to be typical of the numerous other, less well-preserved drainage mills dotted across the marsh. But in one important respect it is not. It was not built as a drainage mill at all. Its original function, when constructed in the 1860s, was to grind clinker for the cement works at Reedham. It was converted to use as a drainage mill in 1880 and that is why, unusually, it has its scoop wheel in a separate building added on one side, rather than within the tower.

By the eighteenth century, the management of the marshes was similar to that still practised in many parts today. By this date cattle, which had been grazed on the marshes since at least late medieval times, had largely replaced sheep. In spring the animals were put out to graze after the 'freeboard' in the dykes had been set to a height of about two feet, allowing the dyke to fill with water. This provided the animals with drink and prevented them from straying from one area of marsh to another. In autumn, the animals were taken off and the water level lowered, in order to provide as much storage capacity as possible ready for the winter rains.

Today, the maintenance of the dykes is carried out by machinery, but well into the twentieth century everything was done by hand. The marshman raked out mud and decaying

The Berney Arms windpump.

waterweed with a 'crome' (an implement resembling a fork with the end of the tines bent at right angles), and trimmed the marginal vegetation with a scythe or a side-cutter. Every few years more extensive work, known as 'bottomfying', had to be carried out. A short section of a dyke was dammed, the water bailed out and the sediment that had collected to the depth of a metre or more removed. The mud was spread over the nearby ground, and this process gradually gave each section of marsh the form of a shallow saucer. This in turn necessitated the digging of further shallow 'foot-drains', with turf cutter and wooden spade, in order to bring water from the centre of the marsh to the main drains.

When the Angles Way leaves the flood wall it passes up the side of Burgh Castle staithe. Staithes or landing places such as this were vital to the life of riverside parishes in the past when most heavy goods were transported by water. Most of the villages beside the Broads and marshes in this part of East Anglia had one. From here, the Way climbs on to the higher ground by the church of St. Peter and St. Paul. This church, although pleasant enough, is not particularly distinguished in historical or architectural terms. But it has an important feature which it shares with many along the course of the Angles Way: it has a round tower. Such towers are almost entirely restricted to the area between the Thames and the Wash, and the great majority (over 160) are situated in Norfolk and Suffolk, with the densest concentrations occurring in the valleys of the rivers Waveney and Yare. As with any unusual or distinctive feature, theories abound about their age and purpose. The most picturesque is that they were not originally built as towers at all, but are the remains of ancient wells, the surrounding soil having been washed away by Noah's flood!

More serious consideration has been given to the suggestion that they were built as defensive structures, their shape standing up better than a square tower to battering from without. According to this theory, the towers originally stood alone, and the churches were a later addition. They are built in defensible situations in response to a specific threat, probably the Viking invasions in the ninth century. There is, however, little if any evidence to support these suggestions. In particular, the structural evidence usually, if not invariably, suggests that the towers are either contemporary with their churches or a later addition. Some round-towered churches may be situated in potentially defensible positions, but so too are many with square towers. As to being a response to a particular threat, the problem here is that, unlike the superficially similar freestone towers of Ireland, flint towers cannot be erected in a single season. On the contrary: flint rubble construction is a slow business, with a height of three metres per year probably being the maximum possible in the early Middle Ages. It is, moreover, difficult to see what such a threat might have been. Certainly, it cannot have been the Vikings, even though the coastal and riverine distribution of the towers might, on the face of it, appear to lend some support to this suggestion. Recent research suggests that the earliest towers were built at the very end of the Saxon period, after the period of Viking raiding, and that the majority were probably constructed during the century following the Norman Conquest.

A more sophisticated version of the 'defensive' theory argues that these structures could have combined a defensive function with that of church tower. But the problem here is that the thatched roofs of the churches would have been very easy to set on fire, and the smoke would then have been drawn into the tower as up a chimney, suffocating those taking refuge within.

Most archaeologists and architectural historians would reject the 'defensive' theory and argue that the towers were built in this manner for purely practical reasons. The argument goes like this. There is no source of good building stone in East Anglia. Car stone, a form of hard sandstone, is found and used for building in the western parts of Norfolk, but across most of the region the only available stone is flint, which occurs in the boulder clay, and in the underlying chalk. It is difficult to form corners or openings from these small, irregular nodules, and for these medieval church builders usually obtained freestone from outside the region - usually limestone from France, or from Northamptonshire on the far side of the Fens. The individuals or communities who built these early churches, however, may have had insufficient resources to provide freestone for both the corners of the main structure of the church *and* the tower. The corners of the main body of the church had to be square: but the towers could be circular in plan.

Many people accept this sensible explanation, but it is not quite as straightforward as it first appears. It is, in fact, possible to build square towers without freestone corners. There are a number of examples in Norfolk, including those at Heigham, Hethel and Weybourne. It is also questionable whether the problems involved in constructing such a tower would really outweigh those involved in laying out a round tower, and in incorporating it with the straight gable wall of the nave.

An entirely different explanation has been put forward by
Stephen Heywood, who argues that no practical explanation is
needed. He points out that there is another area of northern
Europe in which round towers are common - northern Germany,
particularly Schleswig-Holstein and the area immediately to its
south-east. In this area the towers are built of freestone, so that
arguments relating to the practicalities of building do not apply.
He suggests that here the builders and patrons simply preferred
round towers for aesthetic reasons; and that trading links, and
consequent cultural links, led to a similar preference in East
Anglia. Such trading links have so far only really been
established with the areas around the Wash where, unfortunately,
round towers are largely absent. Moreover, it is difficult to judge
whether the similarities between the towers in the two regions,
such as the common use in both of double splayed windows,
really outweigh the differences. These include the use in
Germany of square vaulted ground floors, western doors, and
stairs in the thickness of the wall - all features which are entirely
absent from East Anglia.

For what it is worth, our own view is that the truth may lie somewhere between the second and third of these theories. The idea may owe something to continental influence, but if so, the choice was encouraged by the practical difficulties caused by the shortage in East Anglia of good building stone. Like so many debates in history and archaeology, this one remains unresolved. Readers must choose between these rival views - or, perhaps, suggest their own.

After leaving Burgh Castle church the Angles Way follows a track beside the reed-fringed river until it reaches the gaunt, brooding remains of the Roman fort of Burgh Castle. This has been identified as *Gariannonum*, one of the nine 'forts of the Saxon Shore'. In late Roman times these formed a network of defended sites which, under the command of an official called the 'Count of the Saxon Shore', guarded the estuaries between the Solent and the Wash against Germanic raiders. Some historians, however, believe that these forts may not have originally been built for this purpose, but rather to defend against a possible invasion by the imperial Roman government. In the late third century Carausius, then Count of the Saxon shore, is said by early historians to have run a profitable racket, intercepting Germanic raiders *after* they had looted the countryside inland, and keeping their spoils. When Rome tried to intervene,

One of the massive flint-built bastions of the Roman fort at Burgh Castle.

in 286 AD, he declared himself Emperor of Britain, and a fleet sent against him failed to break his hold. He ruled for seven years, and his murderer and successor, Allectus, for a further three, before legitimate rule was re-established. Although the archaeological evidence is not at present sufficient to establish the fort's precise date, most archaeologists now believe that it - like the other 'Saxon Shore' forts - was probably built in the third century, before Carausius' usurpation. It was, therefore, probably intended from the start as a defence against barbarian raiders.

Whatever its precise political or strategic context, there is no denying that the ruins are impressive. The northern and eastern walls still stand, and much of the partly tumbled south wall can be seen. The ground on which the western wall once stood, however, was eroded long ago by the river, and the wall here has entirely disappeared, although the north-western bastion was discovered in the marsh below when a new dyke was being dug in 1960, and a layer of flint rubble from the walls can sometimes be seen in the dyke-side when the water is low.

The walls stand to their original height, although at least one of their five metres lies buried beneath the present ground level. They are made up of a rubble and mortar core, faced with alternating layers of split flints, and brick or tile. They were constructed by building up a course on both sides, filling the resultant trough with rubble, and capping this with a layer of liquid mortar to form a level platform on which to lay the next course. In some places these mortar layers can clearly be seen where the facing has disappeared. The facing of the lower levels of wall has been robbed for use in buildings elsewhere, but that near the top of the walls is intact, protected by height and, until relatively recently, by a covering of creepers.

At the corners of the fort, and at intervals along the walls, are round bastions which were constructed in a similar way. Although these are not keyed into the walls for their first seven or eight feet, it has been shown that they were built before the walls were completed. Nobody really knows why their bases stand free of the walls in this way. The most likely explanation is that the builders changed their minds during construction. In the top of each bastion is a hole about two feet in diameter. It was once thought that these were for holding a *ballista* - a piece of artillery like a massive cross-bow. It is, however, now thought more likely that they held a post supporting a timber super-structure and roof.

Roman troops ceased to garrison the fort in the late fourth or early fifth century but the result of excavations here suggests that there was some sporadic use of the site thereafter, and a large Anglo-Saxon cremation cemetery lies in the adjacent field. In the seventh century, however, the interior of the fort was reoccupied on a large scale. This may have been associated with the use of the fort as a monastery, established by the Irish Saint Fursa. Bede described this as being 'pleasantly situated in the neighbourhood of woodland and sea, and built in a certain *castrum*'. This last Latin word has usually been translated as 'camp' or 'fort', admirably fitting this location, but by Bede's time the word was used rather more loosely, and could equally refer to a small walled town, leaving a rather wider choice of sites. Between 1958 and 1961 a substantial cemetery was excavated within the fort, from which over a hundred and fifty burials were recovered. These were probably Christian graves, as virtually no grave goods were found. They were all inhumations, and included skeletons of all ages, although with a high proportion of adults - suggesting, perhaps, a combined lay and monastic community. The burials appear to have taken place over a considerable period of time during the Middle Saxon period, and the community which the cemetery served was probably not a large one. The excavations revealed a number of contemporary buildings, but none of an obviously ecclesiastical nature, and their slight remains are difficult to equate with the imposing buildings that Bede tells us were the gift of King Anna and his nobles. Was this, then, Fursa's monastery? The evidence, once again, remains ambiguous, and it must be remembered that the excavations only investigated a comparatively small area within the fort. If this was a monastery, then its location here fits in well with a pattern identified elsewhere in England. As the early Christian missionaries established monasteries and churches within the Anglo-Saxon kingdoms, they often used places with strong Roman associations - military installations, or abandoned walled towns. In so doing, they proclaimed their associations with the classical past, with a culture which had disappeared from England several centuries before.

Whatever the nature of this Anglo-Saxon reoccupation on the site, this was clearly not the end of the fort's active use. In

Norman times, a 'motte', or castle mound, was raised in the south-western corner, and the Roman walls used to enclose a 'bailey' or outer defended enclosure. Many hundreds of 'motte and bailey' castles were built in England in the century following the Norman conquest. The motte, which was originally crowned by a timber watchtower, was levelled in 1839 when the interior of the fort was ploughed.

The Angles Way rejoins the river and soon reaches a large boatyard. This occupies the site of the Burgh Castle Brick and Cement Company, which was set up in 1859. The low, single-story cottage, which stands to the left of the path after it leaves the river bank, was once the company's office. The extensive mooring pools at the southern end of the site, moreover, date from this time. When the company was first set up there were no proper roads leading to the works, and most of its products were transported by water, in the traditional Broadland sailing barges known as wherries. Two types of clay were dug close to the river bank, to produce both red and white bricks, some of which can be seen in the village of Burgh Castle, and also in the Aquarium Theatre on Yarmouth's sea-front. The cement was made from a mixture of mud dredged up from Breydon Water, and chalk brought by wherry from Whitlingham on the River Yare near Norwich. This was fired in kilns that stood in the north-west corner of the site, and then transported to the Berney Arms Mill for grinding. The company, with several changes in ownership, continued in production until the outbreak of the First World War. It was revived after the war, but only for a short period, and producing only bricks, before closing for good in the early 1920s.

Leaving the river the path turns east and soon skirts the edge of Belton, once a quiet rural village but engulfed over the last fifteen years by a vast dormitory development for Yarmouth. This curious eruption of suburbia is, however, soon left behind when the path joins a lane that, long ago, divided the common heaths of the villages of Belton and Fritton. We are now running through the middle of Lothingland, or the *Isle of Lothingland* as it is sometimes called. It must have appeared an island indeed when the marshes to the north were still undrained, when it was a peninsula, only connected to the mainland by a narrow strip of land near Lowestoft. The brickearth deposits on the edge of the river, which the Burgh Castle Company exploited for so long, are a geological anomaly. For the most part Lothingland is covered in sands and gravels, and during the Middle Ages was an area of extensive heaths, interspersed with areas of arable land, worked as open fields. Some areas of the heath were, especially during the sixteenth and seventeenth centuries, used as rabbit warrens. The names 'Fritton Warren' and 'Ashby Warren' still appear on the modern Ordnance Survey map.

The heaths were gradually enclosed and reclaimed between the seventeenth and nineteenth centuries: those of Belton and Fritton disappeared following an Enclosure Act of 1809. But as the path leads westward, some flavour of the long-vanished heathland is provided by the wide bracken-covered verges, with occasional gorse bushes growing amongst the invading scrub. Although the heaths were considered waste land - 'barren deserts' - by the agricultural improvers of the eighteenth and nineteenth centuries, areas to be reclaimed if possible and converted to arable, in earlier times they were valued as a resource in their own right, as a source of grazing, thatching, and fuel in the form of furze and bracken.

When the Angles Way leaves the former common it passes through an area which, as late as the early years of the nineteenth century, still partly consisted of open fields, divided into large numbers of separate strips. Finally it reaches Fritton Church. This ancient building gives the walker a rare chance to visualise the kind of church which, in many cases, originally accompanied the round towers of the region. It still has its twelfth-century semi-circular apse at the eastern end, contemporary with or slightly earlier than its round tower. This form of chancel is typical of the period. A squared end only became normal in small churches after changes in religious practice which took place during the thirteenth century. These involved, in particular, the abandonment of the freestanding altar, behind which the officiating priest would stand and face the congregation, and its relocation against the east wall, so that the community would only see his back. The porch and all the larger windows are later additions, and the nave has been heightened and extended to the south, but the observer needs only to remove these few details in her or his mind's eye, and add one or two more small lancet windows, to envisage the building's original form.

But Fritton church is not only interesting in terms of its architecture. Its location is also worth considering, for it is the first of several churches on or close to the Angles Way which stand isolated from the houses of the parish. Early maps show that the other buildings of the village stood beside areas of common land, some beside the marshes, others next to small greens on the higher ground. This pattern is repeated again and again in East Anglia. Where archaeological studies have been made they show that in Saxon times the houses of the village clustered around the church. They drifted away, to common-edge locations, during the eleventh and twelfth centuries. Nobody really knows why: but it might have had something to do with the great increase in the population which was occurring at this time. Pasture land was put to the plough, and this put a premium on the common grazing lands, and made it important for each farmer to stake his claim to them. For without pasture, there was no way of maintaining oxen to pull the ploughs, cows to provide milk, or other necessary stock. East Anglia was, at this time, an area in which farming was organised on a fairly individual basis, and one in which there was an active market in peasant land. It seems likely that farmers bought, sold and exchanged land in order to gain a foothold on the edge of the common. A dwelling here would give the best opportunity of exploiting your right to use the common, and of preventing its unauthorised or excessive exploitation by others. This, at least, is one current theory. Unfortunately for historians, the great common-edge migration occurred before detailed records were kept, so its causes must remain a matter for speculation rather than certainty. It has certainly left its mark on the landscape, not only in the form of isolated churches, but also in the scattered, dispersed nature of the settlement pattern. Yet it is not always obvious from the present landscape that these houses once stood beside commons. This is because most commons were enclosed, and divided between the local freeholders, after the Middle Ages. This was often, as at Belton and Fritton, as the result of a Parliamentary Act, during or soon after the Napoleonic Wars. Grain prices were very high at this time, and this encouraged the conversion of these rough grazing lands to arable.

3. Decoys, Broads, and a Great Estate

On leaving Fritton church, the path skirts the end of Fritton lake. Although this area of water is not actually visible from the Angles Way, it can be reached by making a short detour, through the Country Park to the east of the church. Such a detour is well worth the effort. Not only is the lake, encircled by woodland, an impressive sight. It also brings us into contact with an activity which was once common in East Anglia, but which has now vanished almost without trace. For the old name for this area of water was Fritton Decoy, after a method of wildfowling used on a large scale here in the eighteenth and nineteenth centuries.

The capture of wildfowl had long been a part of the economy of the wetland areas of East Anglia, but the introduction from Holland of a new method of netting the birds, first recorded in the 1620s, allowed a more systematic exploitation of this important food source. A 'decoy' - the word is derived from the Dutch *eende kooi* meaning 'duck cage' - consisted of a series of 'pipes', curved, tapering inlets about 75 metres long, leading off from an area of open water. These were dug to a depth of about 50cm, and were covered, after the first seven or eight metres, with nets supported by hoops of decreasing height. On the inner landward side a series of reed fences was erected, arranged *en echelon*. The netted end of the pipe was hidden from view of the open water by vegetation, but the banks around the open end were kept free of plant growth, in order to encourage the birds (chiefly Mallard and Teal) to congregate there. They were then

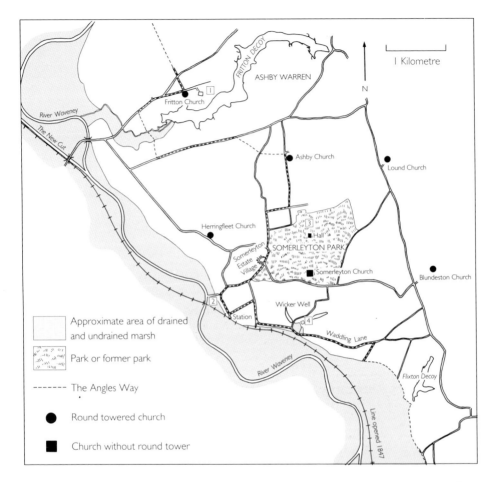

1 Kilometre

N

FRITTON DECOY

ASHBY WARREN

Fritton Church

River Waveney

The New Cut

Ashby Church

Lound Church

Heringfleet Church

SOMERLEYTON PARK

Somerleyton Estate Village

Hall

Somerleyton Church

Blundeston Church

Wicker Well

Station

Waddling Lane

River Waveney

Flixton Decoy

Line opened 1847

Approximate area of drained and undrained marsh

Park or former park

The Angles Way

Round towered church

Church without round tower

1	Fritton Country Park
2	Wherry Cut and former brickyard
3	Site of 17th century Italianate Garden
4	Site of 17th century water garden

lured into the nets by tame birds, or trained dogs, or most often by a combination of the two. A tame duck, accustomed to being fed near the mouth of the pipe, was attracted by the decoyman's quiet whistle, to be followed by other birds. The dog would then show itself, running around one of the reed screens. The birds, viewing this from the end of the pipe, would see something resembling an appearing and disappearing dog. Contrary to expectations, and for reasons which have never been fully explained, they would swim towards this apparition. The dog would then repeat the manoeuvre, running around the next screen in the sequence, and so on, drawing the birds ever further into the pipe, until, when they were out of view of the main water, the decoyman would show himself behind them and drive them into the narrow end or 'purse' of the net. Here they could be extracted and silently dispatched, out of sight of other birds on the open water, which could therefore be trapped later in the same way. The nets and screens have, of course, all disappeared long ago, but the location of some of the pipes can still be seen, as blunt inlets or reed patches in the side of the lake.

Some decoys were made on purpose-built areas of water, but many, like those at Fritton Lake and at Flixton Decoy, which we shall pass a few kilometres further on, were made by adapting the shores of waters already in existence. A successful decoy required a number of pipes, as the birds congregated on the sheltered side of the water and preferred to swim into the wind, so the decoyman needed to be able to select a pipe according to conditions. Even so, the catch depended greatly upon weather conditions, and on the skill of the decoyman, not least in avoiding arousing the suspicion of the other birds in the vicinity.

Fritton Decoy, showing one of the 'pipes' when still in use in the early years of this century.

The method worked best for migratory birds which were new arrivals in the country, and to which the appearance of the dog was a novelty.

Large numbers of decoys were created throughout East Anglia in the years between the Restoration and the first decades of the nineteenth century. They were usually leased out to professional decoymen. Flixton decoy appears always to have been in single ownership, but at Fritton at least half a dozen men owned pipes by the end of the eighteenth century. The decoy at Flixton is particularly important since it was one of the earliest to be created in the country - it was already in full operation by 1652. That at Fritton, on the other hand, whose early history is unrecorded, was one of the last to remain in use, still being worked in the first decade of this century. In 1909, east coast naturalist Arthur H. Patterson described an unsuccessful day's decoying here.

> From behind my peep-hole in the reeds I could see without being seen. I saw that the dog was exceedingly eager - for a bit of bread; and no sooner had he jumped one barrier, and come back over the next, than he opened his jaws ready for the thrown morsel. He scampered over one barrier after another; but the ducks, although turning their heads, refused to be decoyed. Ducks usually betray much curiosity over the decoy dog's manoeuvres, and with outstretched necks they follow him eagerly; but to-day they were obdurate. We did little on this occasion; the dog and decoyman did badly - I did worse! for

Flixton Water: detail from an estate map of 1652, showing the netted decoy 'pipes'. This is one of the earliest known representations of a duck decoy in England.

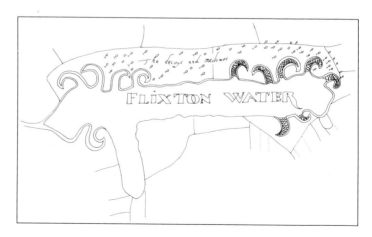

being overcome by curiosity, I peered behind the screen looking *up* the pipe, forgetting that there were scores of fowl *outside* it. With a roar of wings and many a frightened quack! up flew fifty or sixty fowl alarmed at such an apparition.

By this date, Fritton was a rare survival. During the second half of the nineteenth century decoys ceased to be a viable commercial proposition. There was a great reduction in the size of the catches being made, due to changes in agricultural techniques (especially land drainage), and to the increasing difficulties of providing the quiet environment needed, especially with the growing popularity of wildfowling as a sport. At the same time, the prices to be obtained for mallard, teal and other wildfowl were falling due to cheap imports from Holland and France, and to the increasing market in English game birds.

Although taking its name from it use as a decoy, this area of water has a much longer history. It is one of a large number of similar lakes which are found in the valleys of the rivers in east Norfolk and north-east Suffolk, lakes which are locally known as 'broads', and which give this district its popular name - 'Broadland'. They come in all shapes and sizes, and were for a long time assumed to be natural features and, as such, something of a geographical mystery. It is now known that they are, in fact, man-made. Broadland is one of the earliest industrial landscapes in England, for the broads are the flooded remains of medieval peat diggings or *turbaries*. Nobody knows when the excavation of peat on such a vast scale began, but it was going strong by 1200, and may well have started before the Norman conquest. The peat was mainly used for burning, and the intensity with which it was exploited is a clear indication of both the density of population in the area in the early Middle Ages, and the comparative absence of woodland, which might have provided an alternative source of fuel. This bog peat would have become much more dense on drying than that which is sold in bags by garden centres, and burned in a manner similar to that of coal. Some people may find it hard to believe that a lake the size of Fritton could be created by local people digging peat, by hand, with spades. But calculations based on fourteenth-century tithe records, on estimates of the local population during the Middle Ages, and on more recent hand digging rates, have demonstrated that Fritton Lake could quite easily have been created by the people living in the surrounding parishes over a period of about three hundred years.

The broads became flooded during the fourteenth century, due to the continued rise in sea level and climatic change. Their origins were soon forgotten, until rediscovered by research in the last thirty years. The Angles Way passes close to several other broads further along its route. These range in size from the small lake at Wicker Well, one of the smallest areas of water created in this way; through Flixton Decoy, a broad of middling size; to Oulton Broad which is, like Fritton, one of the largest. The broads are an object lesson in the way that even the most apparently 'natural' features in the English landscape can, in fact, be the result of human activity.

In the opening chapter we described how, from the end of the middle ages, the lighter lands of East Anglia came to be dominated by great estates. The area of Lothingland through which the Angles Way now passes was no exception, and by the middle of the seventeenth century large areas were already owned by the Wentworth family, of Somerleyton Hall. We know this because of the survival of a remarkable map, dated 1652, which shows the extent of their estate at this time, and which also tells us a great deal about the appearance of the contemporary landscape. The estate extended into four parishes. Ashby was almost entirely in the hands of the Wentworths. It was largely occupied by heaths and warrens, but most of the arable land was already enclosed - the slightly sinuous outline of the fields suggesting that they had been created by the piecemeal acquisition and hedging of bundles of open-field strips. The Angles Way passes through the middle of this early-enclosed arable land, near Ashby church. The estate continued in an uninterrupted band down the eastern side of the next parish to the south, Somerleyton. The area to the west of Somerleyton church, however, was still being consolidated and enclosed from the open fields, and here the Wentworths' holdings were more limited, and more mingled with those of other men. Still further to the west lay an extensive common, and beyond this, in the low-lying land beside the Waveney, an area of marsh, most of it already enclosed and owned by the Wentworths.

To the south, in Flixton, the Wentworths owned a sizeable chunk of land in the north of the parish, including the decoy, but in Blundeston, to the north-east, their holdings were again more

splintered, and intermixed with those of other proprietors. Thus, while the estate was not entirely continuous, it was surprisingly consolidated for the period.

The house that lay at the heart of this estate was, as we might expect, an impressive one. Later illustrations show that it had shaped gables and up-to-date classical details. But even more striking were its gardens and grounds. The house lay within an extensive deer park - the map depicts a herd of deer grazing in the northern part of the park, and a mounted huntsman with hounds is shown in the south, hotly pursuing a stag (page 45). Parks like this were expensive to create and maintain, and were a mark of wealth and status. Parks had been a common feature of the landscape of East Anglia since the twelfth century, but it is probable that this one was not very old when the map was surveyed. The map shows a road running east-west in the direction of the hall, which comes to an abrupt end at the park pale. The surveyor, not surprisingly, found that this road was 'now entirely out of use', but it was clearly still in evidence, suggesting that it had only recently been closed by the creation of the park.

Perhaps the most remarkable feature of the gardens was the fact that they were 'Italianate' in style: that is, they were modelled on the kinds of gardens laid out around contemporary villas in Italy. Somerleyton is one of only a handful of gardens of this type known to have existed in East Anglia. Indeed, the Somerleyton gardens were, at the time, among the most impressive in England. In Fuller's *Worthies of England*, published in 1662, they are described as being one of the three greatest gardens in Suffolk.

Although the 'Grand Tour' did not become an obligatory part of the education of young men of good birth until the following century, visits to Europe were not uncommon in the seventeenth century, and it is quite possible that Sir John Wentworth had personally seen some of the models on which his gardens were based. The garden stretched from the hall to beyond the northern boundary of the present park, and east to the point where the Way leaves the road from Ashby church (the road at this date continued directly southwards along the then western boundary of the grounds). A plan of the garden appears on the map, and a schedule of 1663 provides some extra details. All the essential elements of an Italianate garden were here. The gardens are set out on a single axis of symmetry at right angles to the house, and were arranged either side of a broad north-south walk. They became progressively larger and more irregular with increasing distance from the house. The sequence began immediately to the north of the house with the rigidly geometric Great Garden. Beyond was the Orchard 'with the Terrace Walk at the south end thereof with the Banqueting Houses upon it', and beyond this a large square area planted with fir trees, called the 'Firrendale' or 'Fir Yard'. This was described by the surveyor as being 'of late the most incomparable piece in the Realm of England, but now ruinated by a great wind'. He tells us that it was planted in 1612 with 256 fir trees, a date at which the ornamental planting of conifers was still a relatively new idea in this country. Fuller was also struck by this particular novelty, commenting that 'here *summer* is to be seen in the depths of *winter* in the pleasant walks, beset on both sides with fir trees green all the year long'. The large area north of the Fir Yard is described as 'the Wood and Walks with a variety of seats, statues, fish ponds, a house for pleasure newly erected and diverse other rarities'. We need to look at the map to gain some idea of its complexity. The wood with its serpentine walks provides the final stage of increasing irregularity, taking informality to a degree unusual in garden design at this early date. To the east of this 'wilderness' area was a water garden, another essential element of Italianate landscape design, with ornamental fish ponds flanked by statues and fountains. The map even mentions a grotto to the north of these - a very Italian feature.

We can look in vain for these gardens today. They have vanished almost without trace. Only a few earthworks show where they once lay, most notably two massive banks just to the north of the present hall, which represent the remains of the 'terrace walk...with Banquetting houses upon it', mentioned in the 1663 schedule. Their disappearance is not due to the poverty of the estate (although its fortunes do seem to have waned during the eighteenth century), but rather to changes in taste. During the second half of the eighteenth century geometric gardens like these became unfashionable. The *à la mode* country house stood in the midst of open, 'natural' parkland, with grass sweeping uninterrupted to its walls.

But fashions in landscape design came almost full circle, and during the early decades of the nineteenth century gardens, rather than just parks, once more became popular as a setting for the country house. A variety of styles was fashionable. Most took their inspiration from the past, and some looked back to the gardens of Italian renaissance villas. The fortunes of the Somerleyton estate also changed in the middle years of the century. A new owner arrived on the scene, keen to make an impact on the landscape.

And so it was that another great Italianate garden appeared around Somerleyton Hall in the 1840s. This offered a slightly different interpretation of the same basic theme - with less emphasis on the single axis or the gradually increasing irregularity, but more on terraces and statuary. This new garden, which was the work of the famous designer W.A. Nesfield, still survives, and has been excellently restored in recent years. It was laid out around a brand new Somerleyton Hall, which also looked back to the past for inspiration - like so much Victorian architecture. In the words of one famous art historian, it is 'more Jacobean than any original Jacobean house'. This is rather ironic because, sealed and hidden away within the more modern structure, are the remains of the real seventeenth-century house which accompanied the great gardens shown on the early map. This was not entirely demolished, and the Victorian house seems to have perpetuated part of its basic plan.

Both house and garden are an extravagant monument to the success of the new owner of the Somerleyton estate: Morton Peto. Peto began life as a bricklayer; by the age of thirty owned a flourishing construction business; and later branched out into railways, taking on work in Argentina, Africa, Australia, Canada, France, Norway, and Russia. He was a shining example of the nineteenth-century 'rags-to-riches' entrepreneur. He became an MP, and was knighted in 1855. In 1866 he went bankrupt. The great house, with its elaborate gardens and surrounding estate land, was sold, lock, stock and barrel, to Sir Francis Crossley. Somerleyton Hall is not clearly visible from the path of the Angles Way. Like most grand dwellings of the eighteenth and nineteenth centuries, it is isolated within an extensive landscape park. This was also created by Peto, and was larger than the earlier deer park, extending much further to the south and west. Several roads and footpaths were diverted and this is why, when the public road which the Angles Way follows reaches the boundary of the park, it makes an abrupt turn to the right. Originally it went straight on: but what landowner would want to spend a fortune on house, garden, and park, only to have the local populace wandering by at all hours, in full view of the front windows?

Peto was not content merely to build and plant within the newly-expanded boundary of his park. His activities spilled out into the surrounding landscape, and, in particular, affected the very fabric of Somerleyton village. Here, Peto changed the plan of the existing settlement and built the striking estate village which stands here today. The architect was probably John Thomas, who was responsible for the hall itself. The village was not entirely new. It was, in fact, an addition to the existing settle-ment, largely built on the former village green, which had been enclosed in 1803. The older buildings still stand in a gently curving line, back from the road, marking the old common edge.

Planned estate villages first appeared early in the eighteenth century, when they were created in order to remove the village to a position where it would not blemish the prospects from the hall or park. By the end of the century, however, they had become an element in the estate landscape, and served to display the landowner's knowledge of current fashion and taste. Leading architects were often called in to design them. Early examples usually show classical influence, but by the early nineteenth century an entirely different style had become almost compulsory - the picturesque. Through the writings of Uvedale Price and of William Gilpin, a formula had been worked out by which the appearance of the country house, its grounds and its estate village could be carefully manipulated to give an impression of natural harmony. The villages were given a kind

Somerleyton: the picturesque estate village and *(above)* thatch and 'Tudor' chimneys.

(Opposite)
The river Waveney and the marshes near Somerleyton. The estate village can be seen in the top left hand corner: the southern part of the park lies to its right. The areas of water to the south of this, 'Wicker Well' and 'Summerhouse Water', were part of an elaborate detached water-garden in the seven-teenth century. Traces of the garden terraces can just be seen in the area of pasture between them.

of 'vernacular' appearance - beams, thatch, porches and the rest - to symbolise a happy rural England, watched over by the benevolent squire. But Somerleyton was not all sham and hypocrisy. Greater than usual consideration seems to have been given to the fact that the village was actually going to be lived in. The dwellings conform to the picturesque in their arrangement around a green, and in the use of a variety of pseudo-vernacular styles, with overhanging thatch or decorative barge-boards and large ornate chimneys. But they are larger than most estate cottages, and storage space is provided internally rather than as the series of lean-tos and sheds which the designer John Nash felt was essential to the picturesque effect. This penchant on the part of Nash had been fully realised at Blaise Hamlet, near Bristol, a famous picturesque village which may, in part, have served as a model for Somerleyton. Similarly, the picturesque properties of the well on the village green were foregone at Somerleyton in favour of a more practical pump. A school was also built, and a new church was planned, although this was never constructed.

But paternalism in this era did not only concern itself with the *convenience* of the inhabitants, as we can see from a description of the village given in the catalogue which accompa-nied the sale of the estate in 1866. The cottages are praised as 'showing, in the Domestic Arrangement and in the Sleeping Apartments, a singular and rare attention to the comfort and morality of Peasant Families'!

By the 1850s, when Somerleyton village was built, the image of the happy rural community was becoming increasingly at odds with the reality of a complex, industrial society, and of a countryside inhabited by impoverished landless labourers, rather than sturdy independent 'peasants'. Landowners like Peto were creating an escapist myth of a happy and contented countryside. Peto, after all, had made his money in commerce, and the estate itself - like many in the period - included a number of industrial enterprises. Indeed, as the footpath leaves Somerleyton village

and turns southwards, it passes through the site of a former brickyard, now occupied by a boatyard. This was active from the beginning of the nineteenth century until 1939, and its products were used to build Somerleyton Hall. They were also used much further afield, in particular in the construction of Liverpool Street Station in London. Bricks were carried down the River Waveney by wherries, even after the coming of the railways, and the cut now used by the boatyard was originally created for these.

The path turns east again at the entrance to Somerleyton station - also constructed of bricks made at the yards we have just passed. The rail line here was owned and built by Peto, and the station is a fairly elaborate affair, to fit in with the estate landscape, and carries Peto's coat of arms. The Way then follows a road across what was once part of Somerleyton common to turn southwards, at what was in the seventeenth century the common edge, on to an old track called Waddling Lane. This follows the edge of the higher ground, along the perimeter of the grazing marshes. Here, where another track meets the Way, on the edges of the parishes of Somerleyton and Blundeston, are two small broads. These had, like Fritton Lake, originated in the Middle Ages as turbaries, but by the time the map of 1652 was made they had been converted into an elaborate water garden. This lay over two kilometres from Somerleyton hall, quite detached from the main area of park and gardens, and presumably functioned as a place for outings, *al fresco* entertainment, and picnics. There were a number of separate ponds here, some with islands on which ornamental buildings stood. One of the ponds bordered the Way, and it can still be seen during dry periods as an area of lush marsh vegetation which contrasts with the coarser grasses around. A short detour up the side lane here, to a point just beyond the cottages, will reveal a square marshy area which marks the site of the second pond, while the steep slope behind it represents the remains of a terrace, along which ran a series of gravelled walks. East of this, more ponds led to a

Somerleyton: the railway station.

'round mount', while on an island in the broad beyond the trees was a small pavilion. Two larger buildings faced one another at the entrance to the gardens, on the site of the present cottages. One of these was leased to a farmer in 1663, but had probably been built as a garden pavilion.

The Way soon leaves the track, continuing along the marsh edge. Passing through an area of wet woodland, it then crosses a stream that drains from Flixton Decoy (the 1652 estate map shows, quite distinctly, the decoy's netted pipes here). Skirting the village of Oulton and passing its church - unusual in this region in having a central tower, situated over the crossing, instead of having one at the west end - the path crosses a deep railway cutting and arrives at Oulton Broad.

This railway was the creation of none other than that great entrepreneur, Morton Peto. It was opened in 1847, in spite of passionate opposition from the famous author George Borrow, then a local magistrate. Borrow's objections were personal, for down the track that leaves the road on the south side of the bridge is the site of the remote cottage in which he spent the second half of his life, and in which he died in 1881. It was here, in a summer-house in the garden overlooking Oulton Broad, that he wrote his best known works, 'Lavengro' and 'Romany Rye'. These were based on his travels through rural England in the 1820s, in the company of the gypsies whom he was later to invite to camp on his land beside the Broad. The railway brought an additional threat to this peaceful refuge, then only accessible by land by means of a footpath, at a time when the reclusive Borrow must already have been anxiously watching the rapid expansion of the settlement of Oulton Broad at the other end of the water. This had hardly existed before the creation of the Lowestoft and Norwich Navigation in the 1830s. Since Borrow's time it has taken over all the intervening land, and the Angles Way passes through some fairly featureless suburban streets. Here, it is something of a relief to come upon a converted malt-house. But it is worth remembering that this structure, attractive to us, was seen in a rather different light when newly built. W.A. Dutt, who wrote several books on the Broads, described it in the 1920s as 'huge and ugly' and, together with the new housing, as having 'robbed Oulton of the beauty it once possessed'.

4. From Oulton Broad to Beccles

The Way emerges from the buildings to cross Mutford Bridge, with Oulton Broad on one side and Lake Lothing on the other. Beneath the bridge is Mutford Lock, an essential part of the Lowestoft and Norwich Navigation. This scheme was carried out between 1828 and 1833 to provide Lowestoft with a safe harbour, and Norwich with access for coastal vessels which avoided the high tolls being charged at Yarmouth. The first part of the scheme involved the cutting of a channel, 500 metres long, to link the then fresh-water Lake Lothing with the sea. This idea had been considered as early as the sixteenth century, when a survey of Lothingland made for Queen Elizabeth mentioned that:

> The main sea...meeteth [the river waters] within a flighte-shoote where the ground is verie low and...may as it seemeth in a short space be cut through again without any great charge.

But no attempt was made to do this before the nineteenth century. When the cut was opened, and the salt and fresh waters mingled, some strange sights were seen - if all the contemporary accounts can be believed. The waters became brilliantly phosphorescent and the surface was thickly covered with the bodies of pike, carp, perch, bream, roach and dace, many of which were later thrown up on the beach having been bitten in two by dogfish. A twenty pound pike, picked up near the bridge, was reputedly found to contain a whole herring!

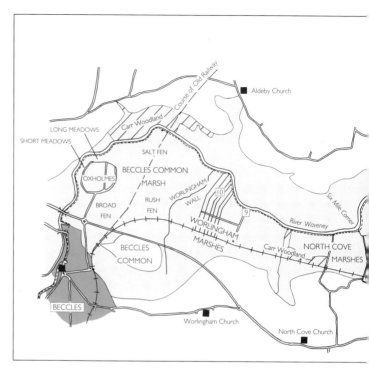

The channel was carried out to sea by building the waters up behind a sea-lock at the top of the cut, then letting them out in a rush,

> Carrying stones, silth, and shingle with a bubbling roar of waters to the ocean, the impetus of which might be distinctly perceived at least half a mile from the shore....The effect of the first sluiceing was such as to sweep out with one rush of the mighty torrent upwards of three thousand tons of beach and shingle into the ocean.

Lake Lothing could now be made into a harbour:

> The Dredger now resumes its usual toil,
> To load the wherries with the muddy soil;
> Forming a spacious harbour in the lake
> For ships to anchor and protection take.

The next stage in the route was the lock through to Oulton

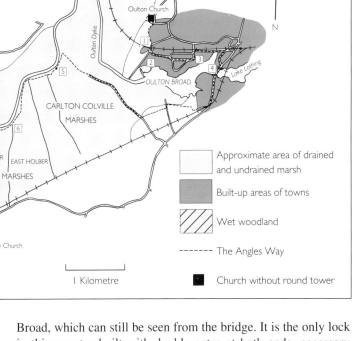

Broad, which can still be seen from the bridge. It is the only lock in this country built with double gates at both ends, necessary because it had a different stretch of tidal water on either side. Pairs of lock gates usually meet in the middle of the lock at a slight angle, forming a point directed towards the higher water level, in order to better withstand its weight. At Oulton, however, the higher water was sometimes on one side, sometimes on the other, for high tide occurs in the Broad about an hour and a half later than in Lake Lothing. Two sets of gates were therefore necessary, in order to stand the alternating pressure. When the height of the water was equal, the gates at both ends could be opened to allow longer vessels to pass through. Shipping then passed through the Broad, along an enlarged Oulton Dyke, and then went down the Waveney as far as St. Olaves. Here it entered the New Cut, which was completed in 1832. This canal, four kilometres long, runs dead straight in a north-westerly direction as far as Reedham, on the river Yare. Its construction ensured that ships could pass directly into that river, without going via Breydon Water and Yarmouth. From this point, only the deepening of sections of the Yare was required to bring vessels as far as the proposed new dock at Norwich.

This 'canal', 50 kilometres long, was opened in 1833, but it soon ran into difficulties. Shipping was becoming larger at this time, and most commercial ocean-going vessels were soon too big for the New Cut. More importantly, the costs of maintaining the new waterway soon outstripped the revenue. The proposed harbour at Norwich was never built, and in 1847 the bankrupt 'navigation' was bought by our friend Sir Morton Peto, partly to eliminate competition to his new railway from Reedham to Lowestoft, but also to facilitate the development of land he owned beside Lowestoft harbour. The New Cut still survives, but is now only used by pleasure craft, the yachting associations having successfully resisted its closure after it was badly damaged by the floods that accompanied the great gale of 1953. Pleasure craft now form a considerable industry in Broadland, and have done so since the 1920s. Nowhere is this more apparent than here on Oulton Broad, densely packed for much of the year with vessels of many kinds.

As the Angles Way leaves Oulton Broad it cuts across the low-lying marshes beside the river. It then follows the course of

(Above) Ships at Mutford lock, c.1920.

(Right) Mutford lock.

the river wall as far as Beccles, affording for most of its length
an uninterrupted and often striking view across the drained
marshes. These, for all their atmosphere of timeless tranquillity,
would be flooded regularly by the tidal river if it were not for
man's constant efforts to exclude the water from them. Like the
more extensive areas of marsh in the area around Breydon
Water, these were probably drained during the early Middle
Ages. As the silting up of the great estuary around Breydon
impeded the flow of the River Waveney, banks of silt built up
here, and peat began to form where areas of water were cut off
from the main flow. Two theories have been put forward
concerning how man first became actively involved in the
banking and dyking of this land. It is possible that, as reserves of
pasture dwindled during the high Middle Ages, banks were built
to keep the river to a narrower course, and so artificially extend
the villages' supplies of grazing land. Alternatively, it has been
suggested that due to the lowering of the level of the sea around
our coasts which occurred during the early Middle Ages, these
marshes may, by the twelfth century, already have stood
sufficiently high and dry to provide grazing for most of the year
without the need for banks. By the late thirteenth century,
however, the sea level was rising again and floods were
beginning to cause serious problems all along the coast. The
Great Flood of 1287, which caused great damage in Yarmouth,
also swamped low-lying land all along the river valleys. Saint
Benet's Abbey, near Ludham on the river Bure, was under
several feet of water, and a similar situation must have occurred
here in the Waveney, where the marshes are at much the same
height above sea level. Sea levels continued to rise over the
following centuries, and although there are no documentary
records of an embankment on this stretch of the river until the

Pleasure craft on
Oulton Broad.

59

sixteenth century, the river wall here must have been in existence long before.

In the Middle Ages, and in some cases as late as the nineteenth century, the marshes were common land, managed by the communities in each parish. They were not divided up into parcels owned and occupied by individuals, but were exploited jointly by the principal proprietors. Unlike less vulnerable commons, this involved shared responsibility for maintenance of flood protection works, as well as shared rights. But for the most part each community, each parish, organised its own drainage and flood-protection schemes. Even the river walls, which run continuously along both sides of the river, were maintained, and probably constructed, in lengths solely by the individual parishes within which they lay. The same was true of the 'walls' or 'dams' running back from these, dividing one community's marsh from the next. These follow most of the parish boundaries, running from the high ground, across the marsh, to join the river wall. They protected each section of drained marsh from floods on neighbouring commons. Two of the most interesting are the Hundred Drain, dividing North Cove from Barnby, and the Worlingham Wall, dividing that parish from Beccles. Both of these follow the winding path of a former natural water course:

Worlingham Wall, a medieval flood defence.

that is, the water course originally formed the parish boundary, but became hemmed in on both sides by the banks separately raised by each parish. A footpath (part of the Beccles Marsh Path) leaves the Angles Way and passes along the top of the Worlingham Wall, providing the opportunity for a closer look for walkers with time to spare. It is noteworthy that no early wall exists between Carlton Colville and Barnby. The Boundary Dyke here was only created around 1800, suggesting that the two parishes originally managed their flood defences together.

The fact that the marshes were 'common' did not mean that they were jointly owned by the commoners. Commons, whether marshland or other forms of grazing, were usually the property of manorial lords, and were 'common' only in that members of the community had the right to use them. At Beccles the situation was unusual, in that here the community paid a rent for the privilege to the manorial lord, the abbot of Bury St. Edmunds. In Henry VI's reign, this amounted to £6 13s 4d *per annum*. This payment ceased, however, after the Dissolution, when the marsh passed to the crown and, after a protracted legal battle, was eventually acquired by the town. From this date, there are detailed records of the way the marshes were exploited and maintained, records which probably provide some indication of the way that other, less well-documented communities in the valley treated their low-lying commons.

The Beccles records provide much information about the maintenance of the extensive banks and dykes. In 1552, in Beccles Common Fen alone, 950 rods - nearly five kilometres - of dykes were 'drawne and skorred' to prevent them becoming choked with weeds. In addition to this work, walls had to be kept in repair and causeways had to be created and maintained to allow access for wheeled vehicles. In the same year two men were paid for making faggots and mowing rushes to lay in a causeway, while a third carried twenty four loads of gravel to the same causeway. These raised gravel tracks can still be seen meeting the footpath at intervals along the river wall, and can be picked out at a greater distance by the rows of gates leading off them, or by the willows growing along their sides.

Both in Beccles, and in other places, the dykes and ditches did not just serve to drain the marshes. They also divided them into separate areas, which communities could use and manage in different ways. In particular, they prevented stock from wandering freely. An undated seventeenth-century document from Carlton Colville describes three small areas of marsh. In Horde Marsh, which covered fifty acres, the inhabitants were 'pasturing their horsebeasts and other cattall all the year', while on the forty acres of Redefenne and ten acres of Slypp Marsh they 'doe use to mowe in somer and with in some tyme after mowinge the grass being growne... doe feed with there cattell'. In other words, a hay crop, essential to provide winter feed for livestock, was taken before animals could be permitted to graze.

Many areas of pasture within the marsh were too wet in winter to allow grazing all year. Thus, for example, in sixteenth-century Beccles no animals were let on to the Salt Fen - a large area below the Angles Way, to the west of Worlingham Wall - until the 3rd of May, to give the grass time to start growing. There were some very boggy patches: an entry in the Beccles Fen Reeves' Account for 1552 refers to the payment of twopence to two men 'for poolying a horse owt of ye moyer'. Some areas would have made poor quality grazing at any time of the year for they were so waterlogged that they were covered in rushes. But even these had their uses. In 1544 it was stated that 'yt shalbe lawfulle to all women inhabiting wythyne the sayd towne of Becclys att all tymes mete and convenyent to go into the sayd fen lande and pasture... to shere and gather (rushes) wythe thyr sykkls... for thyr dressing up of thyr houses'. This probably refers to the use of rushes as a floor covering, but the crop was also important for thatching, and for making lights. Stripped of most of their outer layer to expose the pith, soaked to remove the juices, then dried and dipped in fat, rushes could then be placed in a holder on the wall and lit like a candle.

There were also areas of fen where turfs of peat were cut for fuel in spring and stacked in the open air to dry through the summer. As late as 1762 a part of Rush Fen was set aside 'for cutting of turf for the use of the poor Inhabitants of the said town of Beccles'. We shall meet other such fuel allotments further along the Angles Way.

Parts of the marsh were occupied by 'carr', damp woodland. This would rapidly colonise any unintensively grazed areas of marsh, especially on the margins of the valley floor. The wood cut from these had many uses, but was above all essential for maintaining the banks and dyke sides in the marsh. Carrs still exist today in most of the parishes along the valley, although only those in North Cove lie close to the Angles Way. These have expanded in the direction of the river, but otherwise cover substantially the same area that they did two hundred years ago, and probably long before that. The best view of carr, however, is across the river from Beccles. Here, in Aldeby, a large and probably ancient area beside the river - Stanley Carrs - is now managed as a nature reserve.

Such areas of wet woodland must have looked very different in the past, when they were intensively managed. Today, we can usually find a variety of tree species growing within them. In the past, to judge from the records, most were almost exclusively composed of alder, with some willow. The alders would have been *coppiced*, that is, cut down to near ground level every few years, in order to produce a crop of uniform *poles* - long, straight, relatively thin pieces of wood. This method of management not only ensured that pieces of useful size and shape were produced. It also increased the quantity of wood coming from each area of woodland. The coppices were usually cut at intervals of seven to ten years: thus a document of 1347 mentions an alder grove in Aldeby which was not to be cut for seven years because it had just been felled. Precautions had to be taken to exclude animals from the carrs. If they were allowed to graze on the new shoots sprouting on the stools after they had been cut, their regrowth would be impeded. The documents suggest that some carrs contained coppiced willow. But trees of

Sheep grazing on the marshes near Beccles.

(Opposite)
The complex pattern
of drainage dykes
near Beccles. In the
top left-hand corner,
curving boundaries
define the former
island of Oxholmes.
The long, tree-fringed
bank meandering
through the marshes
in the right of the
picture is the
Worlingham Wall.
The narrow parcels
of marsh to the right
of this, immediately
to the north of the
area of carr wood-
land, are medieval
reclamations. The
other dykes date
from various periods
in the seventeenth,
eighteenth and nine-
teenth centuries.

this kind would normally have been *pollarded:* that is, coppiced a metre or so above the ground, out of reach of grazing animals, so that they could be grown beside tracks or on the open marsh.

Standing on the river wall, rather less than half way from Boathouse Hill (where higher ground meets the river on the opposite bank) to Beccles Quay, and looking to the east, it is still possible to identify some of the features mentioned in the detailed sixteenth-century records for Beccles. Thus, less than fifty metres away, a curving ditch can be seen. This is the western boundary of Oxholmes, a roughly oval area about half a kilometre wide. Although now a fairly featureless area of open grassland, in the sixteenth century this was occupied by a carr, and in the Beccles archives there are many references to the cutting of alder and willow here. The land which lay between here and the river was known as Short Meadows, and was used for raising a hay crop, and for grazing once the hay was in. In the far distance, beyond Oxholmes, lay Beccles Fen, a damper area which was always used as open common pasture.

The communities along the valley had to regulate the number of animals being put out to graze, especially as more intensive animal husbandry became common in the area in the sixteenth and seventeenth centuries. At Beccles, all cattle had to be entered in a 'Warning Book', and those on the marsh were regularly rounded up in a 'drift' to check that only those in the book were present. The spirit of cooperation was not always to the fore, for in 1671 Alborough Williams was fined by the court 'for refusing to have his cattle brought into the drift and for threatening the officer'.

In some ways land use in these marshes was more varied in the past, in some ways it was less so. On the one hand, areas used for turf and peat cutting, and many areas of carr woodland, have disappeared. On the other, large areas of the marsh in Beccles and Carlton are now under the plough. In the Middle Ages, and for long after, the arable land was always situated in other places: the marshes were never used in this way, but instead formed an essential complement to the arable on the higher ground. Now, fortunately, the grazing marshes between Yarmouth and Lopham have been declared an Environmentally Sensitive Area ('ESA'), and farmers encouraged to maintain traditional management practices. Without this policy, it is likely that many more acres of these ancient meadows would have

fallen to the plough over the last three decades or so.

Over the centuries, at different times in different places, the open marshland commons were enclosed, and the common rights over them were eroded or exchanged for exclusive rights over smaller pieces of land. This transition from open common land to enclosed private property has left its mark on the landscape, in the form of the dykes dug to separate the individual parcels. As we have seen, the marsh was never entirely open - there were always dykes for drainage, and for separating areas used in different ways - but in the post-medieval centuries, these proliferated. From different places on the Angles Way, we can see different kinds of enclosure, created by different methods at different times.

Soon after joining the river bank in Carlton Colville, the path skirts an area that remained as a common until the end of the eighteenth century. The western part of Carlton Colville, the whole of Barnby, and that part of North Cove contained within the northerly loop of the river, were all enclosed by Parliamentary Act within a few years of the turn of the nineteenth century. The area is characterised by dykes laid out in the ruled lines typical of Parliamentary Enclosure, although there are a few more sinuous watercourses, where earlier ditches were retained.

The other areas of marsh, as far as the town of Beccles, were enclosed at earlier periods. In the western part of Worlingham parish, clearly visible from the Angles Way, the dykes form a striking pattern, dividing the marsh near Worlingham Wall into a number of long, parallel strips, all of which kink at the same point. Such a pattern looks like the result of a decision taken by a group of commoners to divide the marsh between them, at a stroke. This probably happened in the sixteenth or seventeenth centuries, but might have occurred earlier. In most places, however, enclosure seems to have occurred piecemeal, bit by bit, over a longer period of time, as the wealthier landowners agreed to forgo rights of common in return for an allotment of their own. In Beccles, the first few enclosures in the common marsh came soon after its acquisition by the town in the middle of the sixteenth century. References to enclosures in the town archives increase through the seventeenth and eighteenth centuries, a period in which the reclamation of wetlands and their agricultural improvement were being undertaken on an increasing scale over much of Europe. The last areas had ceased to be open by the 1790s.

The incentive to enclose did not, initially at least, come from any desire to convert the grazing grounds to arable. Indeed, at Beccles, such a course was, at first, expressly prohibited by the terms of leases. The main motive seems to have been to allow for an increase in the amount of meadow land, perhaps indicative of the increasing numbers of stock being kept through the winter in the locality as it became an area specialising in dairy farming. With the high grain prices of the late eighteenth century, however, special permission for ploughing was sometimes given at Beccles, and here, and in other parishes, some of the drier areas of the marsh seem to have been ploughed.

Even after enclosure had been completed on the marsh, the pattern of dykes and ditches did not remain unchanged. Thus, for example, the pattern of long, strip-like enclosures in Worlingham, mentioned above, is sliced through by a later causeway with flanking dykes, visible from the path as a row of gateways. In North Cove, a number of changes within a small area can be followed in documents. By the second decade of the nineteenth century the Hundred Drain had become choked with weeds. The owners of the adjacent areas of marsh decided to dam it, and to take the water off up a new cut. A few years later, one land holder challenged this decision, and after appeal to the court of the King's Bench, was able to get the Hundred Drain reopened. The line of the new cut remains, however, as a track running west from the Hundred Drain to meet the river at Six Mile Bottom (where the river leaves its easterly course, and turns due north).

The nineteenth century saw another kind of intervention in this marshland landscape. A railway line, opened in 1859, divides the marshes beside the river from those further south, and the embankment of another line, that once ran northwards out of Beccles, cuts the Beccles marshes into two. This was opened in 1854. The path crosses the remains of the bridge that once took this across the Waveney, and its piers can be seen partially obstructing the river. And changes continue to occur in the pattern of drainage. In the eastern half of Worlingham, for example, a great many more drainage ditches can be seen than appear on Ordnance Survey 6 inch maps, made earlier this century. In the west of the same parish, on the other hand, one or two of the ditches surveyed then have ceased to carry water, and are now discernible only as slight depressions in the ground.

As in the area of more extensive marshes around Breydon, wind pumps were used here from the eighteenth century. They lifted the water from the dykes, over the river wall, and into the Waveney. Old maps show that a number of these stood on the line of the Angles Way. Carlton Share Mill and Castle Mill in North Cove have disappeared, but their sites are marked by modern pumping houses. Another stood in Barnby, near the present footbridge, where the river turns northwards. All three

were certainly in existence by 1827, when they appear on a navigation map. There were others, not shown on this map, including the 'Marsh Mill' at Worlingham, which appears on a map of 1796. The site of this can still be found, beside the Angles Way, at the mouth of the dyke to the east of the causeway that cuts Worlingham's marshes in two. Two others have disappeared without trace: that at Beccles, and the tower mill at Six Mile Bottom in North Cove, which survived until the 1940s.

During the nineteenth century many of the wind pumps were replaced by more efficient steam pumps. The remains of two of these can be seen from the Angles Way. At Castle Mill in North Cove, through the open side of a brick building, the rusting remnants of the steam engine and pumping gear can still be glimpsed in their original position. Less remains at Share Mill in Carlton Colville. Here, beside the modern pumphouse, the engine has gone but a water channel still passes under the path, and a single gear wheel proclaims itself the work of:

Smithdale & Son Fen Drainage Engineers
Millwrights etc. Ramsey Hunts Acle Norfolk.

5. From Beccles to Bungay

Leaving the common marsh, the Way enters the ancient market town of Beccles. The town was probably founded as a secure market by the Saxon king, Edward the Elder, in the early tenth century, after the defeat of the Danish forces. Situated on a spur of higher ground above the river, its position was ideal for defence and also for trade, which it combined with herring fishing. It soon became the property of the Abbey of Bury St. Edmunds and, by the thirteenth century, had a second market and an annual fair. By the end of the following century, it included among its many tradesmen a 'couper, bakere, smyth, pestour, draper, qwilter, chaloner, skynnere, ledbetere, bowyere, parker, carpenter, cok, webbestere' and 'whelwryte'.

Only the street plan and the great church remain of the medieval town - perhaps the best of the early housing was destroyed in the series of disastrous fires from which it suffered in the late sixteenth and seventeenth centuries, but much has survived of the extensive building that took place over the following hundred years. Northgate, the street by which the Angles Way enters the town, has changed remarkably little in the last two centuries. Ornate 'Dutch' gables often proclaim the seventeenth-century origins of buildings whose classical fronts were added in the following century. Slotted between them are fine Georgian town houses, and more humble cottages, all preserved with little alteration, or intrusion of later structures. Northgate leads to the open space of Old Market, the site of the

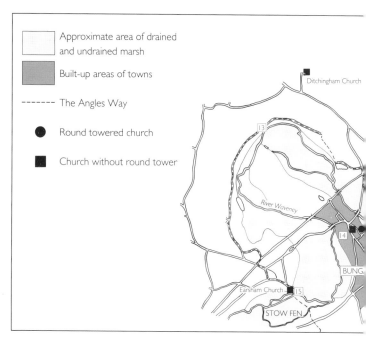

Northgate, Beccles.

original Saxon market place. Here there are more eighteenth-century buildings, and a sole survivor from an earlier period - a timber-framed house, with overhanging jetty, of the late sixteenth or early seventeenth century.

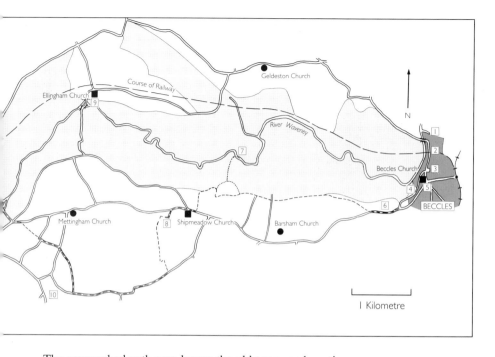

The waymarked path now leaves the old town, and continues under the cliff on which it was built. Numerous alleys, or 'scores', link the streets to the river. Overhead stands the fourteenth-century church of St. Michael, and it is well worth climbing up the cliff steps for a closer look. Here the oddity of the view from the marshes - of a church apparently having a tower at its eastern end, behind the altar - is explained. The sixteenth-century campanile, or bell tower, is not attached to the church, but set slightly to the south east, the usual western position having been rejected by the builders because it was considered 'not safe to build the steepal on the cliffside'. Outside the church, the southern chancel door opens under a rare feature, an external pulpit. There are some fine early gravestones in the churchyard. Immediately below the pulpit, a table tomb has, at either end, a realistic representation of a human skull in deep relief, while on the other side of the path, on a dark grey headstone, another version of this motif appears in the form of a highly stylised deaths-head.

Just beyond the bell tower is the triangular site of the second, or New Market, behind an odd little eighteenth-century town hall

Early eighteenth-century headstones in the churchyard at Beccles: gruesome reminders of mortality.

- a rather early example of a corporate building - which replaced the market cross in 1726. Returning to the cliff bottom, the way-marked path leaves the town on the lower ground by way of Pudding Moor, and signals the fact that we are once again on the valley floor and about to return to the marshes. Skirting their edge for a while, however, we pass Roos Hall, built by the Suckling family in the late sixteenth century, whose great crow-stepped gables and mullioned windows proclaim it a fine example of the architecture of that period.

Leaving the hall behind, the Angles Way runs along the edge of the Barsham marshes - a landscape similar in its appearance, and history, to that through which we have already passed, downstream from Beccles. At Shipmeadow, however, we leave the valley again and head uphill, running for a short distance along the main road and then turning southward. Here, for the first time, we are on the boulder clay, a landscape of wide fields divided, in those places where they still survive, by ancient hedges. Soon we arrive at a building which brings us face to face with one of the less pleasant aspects of the recent past: Shipmeadow workhouse, or 'House of Industry' as it was originally called. This H-shaped building was erected in 1765, at a time when most of eastern Suffolk was rearranging its provision for the poor into 'Incorporated Hundreds', combining the resources of large groups of parishes. The aim was to provide relief more efficiently, and at a lower cost. East Suffolk was the first area in England to experiment with this new method of poor relief. The 'House of Industry' housed the paupers of Wangford Hundred: a unit which contained 27 parishes, running along the Waveney from North Cove to Homersfield and extending to the south in a band four or five miles wide.

The garrets of the top story originally consisted of lodgings for the resident poor - the south wing had two dormitories, girls and single women being lodged in the eastern half and single men and boys in the west. The rest of the garrets were divided into 29 separate rooms for married couples. The lower floors of the northern wing held the Committee Room, and numerous practical offices, including kitchens and a laundry where the 'able women ... are employed in washing, getting up linen and cooking', as well as stores, a dairy and a brewhouse. In the central block, the ground floor consisted of a dining room and surgery, while above these, as well as a workroom, there was a schoolroom where 'the children are taught to read by such paupers maintained in the house as are qualified' - a very rudimentary education, but probably as much as most of them would have received outside. Much of the ground floor of the south wing was occupied by more workrooms and workshops, where the children and less able-bodied women were engaged in spinning wool. The rest of this floor, and virtually all of that above it, was occupied by the Infirmary.

Attached to the workhouse was a small farm of about fifteen hectares. 'Some of the able poor men are employed about the farm and the rest of them let out occasionally to such farmers as are in want of day labourers'. Most of the workhouse land lay in the fields through which the Angles Way passes. Some 300 metres south of the workhouse, in the field to the east, is the ploughed out site of the 'Pest-house', built in 1767, which could house up to thirty paupers suffering from infectious diseases.

The building was still being used as an Isolation Hospital during the First World War.

By the 1830s, population increase and economic depression had led to high rates of rural unemployment, and thus to an escalation in the cost of poor relief, especially in predominantly arable areas like East Anglia. Central government intervened in the administration of poor relief, with economy its foremost aim. The nature of the 'poor' to be provided for had changed, with a much higher proportion of able-bodied people unable to find work. The whole of the country was organised into Poor Law Unions, which aimed both to reduce the cost of provision, and deter potential recipients from accepting relief. Wangford Incorporation became a 'Union', but retained the same boundaries and kept its workhouse. New administrative guide-lines were drawn up. The directors 'found the Diet supplied to the Paupers better in quality and more abundant in quantity than the wages of Industry can procure for a labourer in constant employ' and so prepared cheaper diet sheets. New categories were to be housed, with men and women of 'bad repute' being separated from the others and from the children. A vote was taken among the parishes as to whether married couples should be separated, and although the majority seem to have disapproved of such a move, it was subsequently carried out.

In 1845, a national scandal was sparked off by a riot in the workhouse in Andover in Hampshire. An inquiry revealed that starving men had been fighting over the rotting marrow in bones which they were supposed to be crushing for manure. In 1847, while the controversy continued, Shipmeadow was the scene of a small riot of its own, though with a different cause. It is recorded in the minute book how:

> The Governor reported that during his temporary absence on Monday evening immediately after supper the able-bodied men (instead of returning to their ward) forced themselves into the Girls' Yard - that they then broke a hole in the window of the Able-bodied Women's Ward, all the married men went through and went upstairs with their wives - that they at first refused to attend to his remonstrances, but afterwards yielded to his desire, and went to their own bedroom - that during the above time the schoolboys broke all the windows of the Dining Hall looking into their yard.

The chapel, visible behind the main building as the Way approaches it, was added in 1866. The workhouse remained in use until 1930 when, on the abolition of the Poor Law Board, it passed to the County Council, who mainly used it as a meeting place. Empty in 1938, it came into its own again during the war, first to house a school evacuated from Kent, then to provide residential care for the elderly after bombing in Norwich created a shortage of geriatric beds. After the war it was let to a poultry farmer, and one visitor described seeing turkeys roosting on old bedsteads! It is now in the process of conversion to 'period dwellings'. It is strange to think that a place once so feared by the local population should now become a 'desirable residence' for the middle classes.

Soon after the Angles Way rejoins the road, the walker is offered a choice. A concessionary path follows a track through the fields between ancient hedgerows, but those who stick to the road will pass within a few yards of the ruins of Mettingham Castle and College. In 1342 Sir John de Norwich gained a licence to strengthen his manor house here with walls of stone and lime, and to crenellate it, as a reward for his services in the war with France. He had to return to the war while the building was in its early stages, and it was his wife, Dame Margaret, who completed the work. Mettingham was more of a country house than a castle, like many other fortifications of this period, but the defences were nevertheless impressive. Originally standing at the south east corner of a common called Mettingham Green, the site was surrounded by a series of moats. These are still largely intact, and a section of the curtain wall stands to a height of over six metres, while the three-story gatehouse still guards the entrance. This is built of flint rubble and freestone (brought up the river from Yarmouth to Beccles, then transported overland), with red brick dressings. The groove in which a portcullis was set remains, and the entrances to a gallery above it can be seen. It looks impressive, as its builders intended, but the only time that the castle was attacked the defences proved inadequate, though it may have been largely unoccupied at the time. This was during the popular revolt that followed the introduction of the Poll Tax in 1381, when the castle was taken and ransacked by Jack Straw's insurgents. A year later, only forty years after it had been built, the castle was bequeathed to a college, which already existed at Raveningham in Norfolk, but which moved here soon

after. This was not an educational establishment, but a college in the medieval sense - that is, a group of clerics who said daily masses for the souls of those who had endowed it - and originally contained a master and thirteen chaplains or fellows. By the sixteenth century, however, it was also educating fourteen boys.

The college was surrendered to Henry VIII in 1542, when all such institutions were dissolved, and the buildings were allowed to deteriorate for some years, as a survey of 1562 describes. The lead had been removed from the roof of the gate tower, causing the decay of the 'fayer chamber with a chymney' that had stood above it, and of the 'fayer tower' above that, 'where was a goodlye prospect to view the Townes and villages there aboutes'.

The gatehouse appears to have suffered little further deterioration during the following four centuries, but the internal buildings have disappeared. An elegant chapel had its roof removed in 1542, to cover for a while the old Guildhall at Yarmouth. Part of the main building was still sufficiently habitable in the mid eighteenth century to be converted to a farmhouse, but this was demolished a century later when the present house here was built.

The description of the moated gardens, which were also rather run down by 1562, shows how the master of the college enjoyed a life-style similar to that of a member of the aristocracy. One garden, over an acre in extent, called the 'Inner Ortyarde', was:

> Sett with diverse trees of fruite and devided into sondrye partes with quicksett hedges and quicke hedges of boxe where hathe byn manye fayer Arbors and many small gardens...and hathe fower little pondes in it called fridaye pondes [which] served to preserve fishe taken on [the] weken dayes tyll fridaye.

Leaving this imposing ruin, we can return to the waymarked path. Passing through wide fields - mainly enclosed piecemeal from the open-fields between the fifteenth and seventeenth centuries - we leave the higher ground, and return to the river. Here, at a place called Wainford, we cross the river Waveney for the first time. But, somewhat confusingly, there is not just one watercourse here, but four, crossed by four separate bridges. It is worth pausing a while here, in order to sort out a particularly

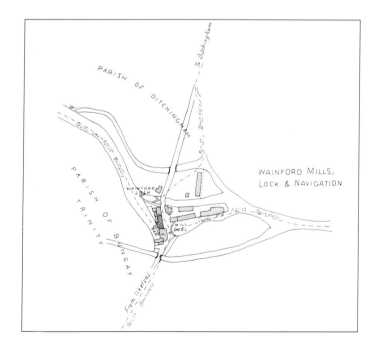

'Wainford Mill, Lock and Navigation' from a map of 1865.

complex piece of landscape.

The first bridge takes us over a tributary, fed by the drainage ditches of the surrounding marshes, which swells the waters of the Waveney a little way downstream. It is the next bridge which crosses the original course of the river, and takes the walker into the county of Norfolk. Yet this is no longer the course taken by the river Waveney itself. The river was dammed here long ago, to work a water mill. The mill pool remains below the bridge, but the mill buildings have gone, corn grinding having long ago given way here to malting.

Today, this is done in a modern automated factory, visible nearby, in the field to the north. The oldest building to the left, before the bridge, however, is the last survivor of seven maltings which were active here at the turn of the century. Facing the road are the windows of the two germinating floors, while the furnaces, with the kilns above them, were situated in the extension behind the north end. Barley was hoisted in sacks to the upper floor and taken into the building through the doorway that can still be seen, and was then placed in the store directly behind. It passed next to the water tanks, or 'steeps', immediately below, where it was soaked for about three days, before being turned onto the first section of the germinating floor. From here it gradually made its way along the floors, being moved every two days or so and turned when necessary, in order to maintain an even temperature. When it had reached just the right stage of germination to produce the particular malt required, it was placed on the perforated tiles of the floor of the kiln to be 'cured', with the temperature being gradually raised over a period of four days to 210 degrees fahrenheit.

Work continued day and night, the barley passing through in a continuous flow, with each grain taking between ten and fourteen days to complete the process. Malting was a highly skilled job, carried out in unpleasant conditions, for the temperature and ventilation were regulated to suit the malt, rather than those who worked with it. It was a trade, however, that fitted well into a rural economy, for since temperatures in mid summer were too great to carry on the process, most of the workforce were released at a time when extra hands were needed for the harvest.

The third bridge at Wainford crosses what is now the main channel of the river. This was almost certainly dug in the 1670s, as part of a scheme to make the Waveney navigable as far as

Bungay. At the time it was stated that 'lighters and keelers and other boats of considerable burden' had in the past been able to reach that town, but due to 'clogging and landing up' of the channel, they could no longer sail above Beccles. Bungay's trade had greatly suffered as a result. It is possible that the construction of large mills like that at Wainford, astride the main channel, had been one factor in restricting navigation. Just upstream from the bridge is the site of Wainford Lock. This was the third of three locks built in the 1670s as part of the scheme. The second was at Ellingham, and the first between Shipmeadow and Geldeston. The latter still retains its waterside pub - a possible place of refreshment for the walker, lying as it does little more than a kilometre from the Angles Way.

The improvement of the river between Beccles and Bungay was, however, only one part of a much more ambitious scheme, which was never carried out. The original idea, suggested in 1670 by one Francis Mathew, was to create a 'Mediterranean Passage' running all the way from Kings Lynn, in west Norfolk, to Yarmouth. This would have involved digging a canal to link the headwaters of the Waveney and Little Ouse, through the

marshy commons around Lopham, Redgrave, and Blo Norton.
The scheme was hopelessly ambitious, and never stood any
serious chance of success, but the Waveney was made navigable
between Beccles and Bungay, and the Little Ouse from Denver
to Thetford, so it was not a complete failure. This section of the
navigation was closed in 1934, and today the Waveney is only
navigable as far as Beccles.

In recent centuries, the vessel most commonly found sailing
the Waveney was East Anglia's distinctive river boat, the
Wherry. Wherries have been recorded on Norfolk rivers since
the beginning of the seventeenth century, but it is in their late
nineteenth-century form that they are best known. The wherry
achieved a great carrying capacity on a shallow draught, because
of the exceptional flair of bow and stern, which provided
buoyancy even when the decks were under water amidships.
This, combined with a very simple rig which allowed the one
great black sail to be hoisted by a single halyard, made it ideally
suited to our shallow rivers. Only one of these boats remains, the
Albion, which was rescued from dereliction in 1949 by the
Norfolk Wherry Trust. She was the only vessel then remaining in

restorable condition. Built in 1898 for a Bungay miller, and capable of carrying a cargo of forty tons, the *Albion* is a typical wherry, except for one important detail - all other wherries had clinker-built hulls, with overlapping boards, while the *Albion* has her boards flush, or carvel-built. This alteration in design was made to enable her to withstand the rather restricted locks between Beccles and Bungay. Even though the boats were not sailed through the locks, but 'quanted' (propelled by poles) with their masts lowered, their clinker-built hulls suffered much damage over time.

The fourth and last of the Wainford bridges crosses a channel with a large sluice at the top. There was originally a weir here, which controlled the water level for both lock and mill. There are eleven water mills along the Waveney: large buildings for the most part, and expensive to construct. The fall in water is so gradual along the river that only the provision of substantial dams, weirs, and sluices made milling by water feasible. The same is true of most rivers in East Anglia, and this - together with the importance of grain-growing in the region from the eighteenth century - explains why there are so many windmills here, compared with parts of western England, where water supplies suitable for milling were much more abundant.

Two kilometres further on, on the outskirts of Bungay, the Way passes another maltings. The large number of maltings encountered in this area is another reflection of the importance of grain-growing in the region during the eighteenth and nineteenth centuries. Still in use, not all of the present structure was built as maltings. The older two-storey block with its blind arcading was

The massive maltings at Ditchingham. These were originally built as a silk mill in 1832, but extended and converted to a new use in the 1890s.

originally a silk factory, erected in 1832 for Grout and Co. of Norwich. Five hundred people were employed here until the 1890s, when the works closed. It was converted to a maltings soon after, by the addition of another substantial block. The result is a more typical example of a nineteenth-century maltings than that remaining at Wainford, with a much more extensive range of malting floors. Like most late nineteenth-century maltings, this once lay close to a railway - an extension, completed in 1863, of the Lowestoft to Beccles line which we passed earlier on the walk, running along beside the Waveney. The arrival of the railways tended to encourage the development of large scale,

The Butter Cross, Bungay.

centralised production of malt at the principal rail heads.

These maltings stand in Ditchingham parish, but they are now on the outskirts of the small country town of Bungay. The Angles Way avoids the town. This is a pity, for Bungay - 'the island of the reed-dwellers' - is an ancient and interesting place. The Way follows the north bank of the river, which turns northwards in a great loop: Bungay, on the south bank, stands on the peninsula so formed. It may have been the site of a late Saxon *burgh*, or defended town, created during the reconquest of the Danelaw. So Ken Penn of the Norfolk Archaeological Unit has recently argued, on the basis of the rather regular street pattern, and the existence of the great earthwork bank (now largely destroyed) which cuts the peninsula off from the land to the south. It was certainly the site of an important stronghold later, after the Norman Conquest, when the Bigods raised the massive castle still visible within the town, with its great gatehouse, thirty metres high and with walls six metres thick. Bungay was already a small town then. It continued to be an important commercial centre throughout the Middle Ages and, like Beccles and many other Suffolk towns, was involved to some extent in the wool trade. It later became more important for linen and later still, during the eighteenth and nineteenth centuries, it functioned primarily as a small market town, supplying a range of services and commodities to its rural hinterland. Does the old local saying 'Go to Bungay and get a new bottom' refer to the use of the local hemp cloth, 'Bungay Canvas', for repairing breeches? Or to the refurbishing of cane seats on chairs? Or to the repair of wherries? All of these things went on in this flourishing town during the eighteenth century. As we saw earlier, the Waveney was once navigable as far as here, and a description of the town in 1813 described the cargoes carried by the wherries:

> Corn, malt, flour, coal, and lime: and several capital flour mills, malting offices, and lime kilns have been lately erected. Here also is a manufactory of Suffolk hempen cloth.

There was a great fire here in 1688, when large areas of the town were burnt to the ground, and the place today has an eighteenth and nineteenth-century feel to it. The decades either side of 1800 were probably its hey-day. The account quoted above goes on to describe;

The principal streets, which are broad, well-paved and lighted...each terminated by a handsome edifice, produce, at first sight, a very favourable impression. The Theatre and Assembly Room are neat structures, and well-frequented, and the county bridge over the Waveney has recently been rebuilt. Here also is a Free Grammar School...and a Meeting-house for Dissenters.

For those not wishing to make a detour into the town, the Angles Way passes close to the site of another feature of the eighteenth-century provincial good life also mentioned in this account:

A pleasant walk of about a mile and a half...conducts to the Bath-house, where there was formerly a vineyard and a physic garden: and it now has an excellent cold bath.

The river has cut back into the clays and glacial gravels as it loops north, so that in places there is quite an impressive cliff. This sheltered, south-facing slope was used by the Bigods as a vineyard in the thirteenth century. The cold bath was established much later, after John King, an apothecary with an eye for a profit, inherited property here in 1721. He discovered a mineral spring, set up the cold bath, and treated a variety of ailments, especially rheumatic. Like most eighteenth-century medicinal bathing places, it also served as a general centre for recreation, with 'Gardens, fruits, shady walks, and all Decorations of a rural Innocance'. The bath - which lay a hundred metres to the east of the building now called the Bath House - was demolished in the 1890s. The spring is still running, however. Analysed in 1944, it was found to contain 'no properties or constituents not common in East Anglian waters'!

There is a magnificent panorama of the grazing marshes here, out towards Bungay. The Way skirts these, and passes the church at Earsham, its great size perhaps reflecting the importance of this place in Saxon times, when it was a royal administrative centre (although the existing fabric is largely of fourteenth- and fifteenth-century date). The path then goes over the meadows and crosses the river by Earsham mill. Beyond the mill is Stow Fen. In the Middle Ages and after, a large number of surrounding parishes - all the Ilketshalls, together with Mettingham and the two parishes of St Mary and Holy Trinity, Bungay - had the right to graze cattle on the lush grass here.

6. The Clayland Landscape: From Bungay to Diss

The path now leaves the valley and the river behind, and climbs up once again on to the boulder clay. Soon we come to a stark, and typically East Anglian, contrast between the very old, and the recent. On the right of the path a vast, empty area opens out to the distance. This is not simply the result of modern hedge-removal. Rather, it is the site of Bungay, or Flixton, airfield. The Second World War made a greater impact on the landscape of East Anglia than on that of any other part of England. Because of their muted terrain and proximity to the European mainland, Norfolk and Suffolk had an incredibly high density of airfields. By the end of the war, there were no less than 71 in the two counties. Indeed, at no point on the course of the Angles Way after it leaves Oulton Broad are you more than ten kilometres from one such feature. These airfields were expensive to build, for each could cost more than £1 million, and this was a very considerable sum in the 1940s. The biggest expansion came after 1942, when the Americans entered the war. By 1944, as many as 4000 or even 5000 flights were being made out of East Anglia each day. Surprisingly little remains of all this investment. Hangars, water towers, huts and control buildings have usually been demolished, and in many cases - as here - even the runways have been quarried away, their material recycled as hard core and the land returned to the plough. Some have become race tracks, some prisons, and many house chicken units or industrial estates. Some, however, like this one, betray their presence only

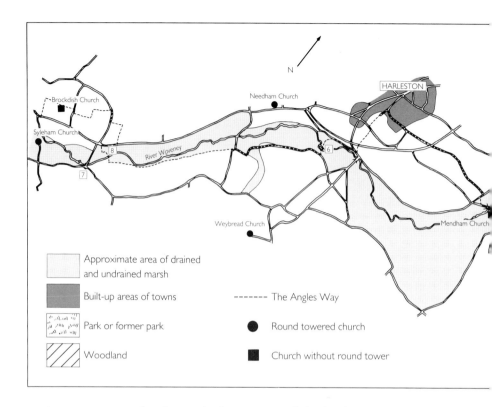

by the marked openness of the landscape, the countryside having been wiped clean of all hedges, copses, ponds and trees when the base was constructed. Work began on Flixton airfield in the summer of 1942, and the first planes arrived in November. It functioned as a 'satellite', or subsidiary station, to Hardwick, some ten kilometres to the north-west, on the other side of the Waveney valley. Several bomber squadrons were based there, including four squadrons of the 446th Bomber Group, the 'Bungay Buckaroos'. It closed in 1945.

South of the airfield, the landscape is almost as bleak, here the consequence of large-scale hedge removal in the 1960s and 70s. The systematic destruction of hedgerows is always unfortunate, but here it is particularly tragic, for the field pattern in this area was one of the most interesting in England. Maps made before the removal of field boundaries began show that these formed a vast, semi-regular grid, extending over the level clay plateau and covering some 45 square kilometres. One of the

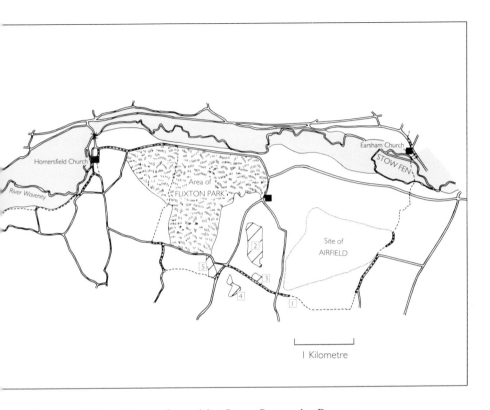

main axes of the grid was formed by Stone Street, the Roman road which runs south from Bungay towards Halesworth. Archaeologists and historians are divided about the antiquity of this apparently planned landscape. The men who laid it out seem to have used the Roman road as a base line, but whether this was in Roman times, or much later, is unclear. Certainly, many of the characteristic features of the medieval landscape appear to have been slotted into an already ancient framework: churchyards, for example, often seem to have been formed from pre-existing fields defined by the grid. Whatever its age, and whatever its purpose, the great field system has undergone many later changes and alterations. Not all the boundaries which survive - or, rather, which survived until recently - are original. Early maps make it clear that, in common with most fields on the clay-lands, these fragmented into strips during the early middle ages, and were only gradually reconsolidated and enclosed in the fifteenth century and later.

Now, however, the landscape has lost much of its historic fabric. Wide fields stretch either side of the path, and only the tattered remnant of a hedge on the left survives as a relic from the middle ages. There is a theory - which has to be treated with considerable caution - that the age of a hedgerow is roughly equivalent to the number of shrub species which it contains in any thirty metre stretch, multiplied by a hundred years. With six or seven species in any thirty metre section - oak, maple, hawthorn, rose, ash, elder and elm - this tattered remnant ought to be around six hundred years old. If so, it was a comparatively late arrival in this ancient landscape.

As the path bends around the southern perimeter of the air-field, it passes the strangely named *Starknaked Farm*. This stands within a moat, or small artificial island, created by digging a roughly rectangular ditch. On the clay soils, such a ditch rapidly fills with water. Many hundreds of these moats were constructed in the twelfth and thirteenth centuries in East Anglia. Indeed, there are at least twenty within five kilometres of this very spot. Some are much larger than this, especially those surrounding the residences of important feudal lords. That at South Elmham, for example, which once surrounded the

A typical view of the East Anglian boulder-clay landscape.

Bishop's Palace (some four kilometres south-west of where we are standing) encloses an area of over a hectare. Many, however, are quite minor features, which surrounded the manor houses of obscure squires, or the homes of prosperous peasant farmers.

Why were they built? It used to be thought that they were primarily defensive in purpose, created to protect residences from attack. But there are problems with this theory. Many moats are not very deep or wide, and can have offered little deterrent to a band of determined men. Some, moreover, seem never to have entirely encircled the house, but only extended along the front and sides. Some historians have suggested that their main purpose was drainage - very necessary on this heavy land - while others have pointed out that they may also have supplied the building materials for the construction of the original house on the site. Other possible uses include the protection of gardens against deer; water supply; sewage disposal; and fish ponds. Yet none of these entirely explains the *form* of the moat, as a wide ditch running *around* the dwelling. Some archaeologists now believe that moats were simply a fashionable form of embellishment. They emulated the truly defensive moats which encircled the great castles of the most powerful barons. They were status symbols, although they also had the kinds of practical uses listed above. And they may well have acted as a deterrent to a casual intruder. Perhaps in a sense they served the same purposes as the burglar alarms, so proudly displayed on the large houses which often stand within them today. They may have helped deter intruders, but they also proclaimed to neighbours that you had something worth stealing!

Continuing along the path, and across the road, we encounter on the right another relic of the medieval clayland landscape: a small ancient wood. It is thick and overgrown now, but peering in through the undergrowth it is possible to see that many of the trees grow up in multiple trunks from a more substantial stump or *stool* near the ground. These are overgrown coppices. For it was not only the alder carrs in the damp valleys which were coppiced. In pre-industrial East Anglia, as in most areas of England, all woods were managed in this way. The amount of woodland was so limited, especially in such a densely-settled and intensively-farmed area as this, that they had to be. Coppices grow very rapidly after they are cut, and thus provided large amounts of wood. This wood was of a shape and size which made it convenient for most everyday uses - tools, roofing timbers, and firewood - without the need for sawing. Only a few of the trees in traditional woods were allowed to grow normally, into large timber trees or *standards*. And even these were seldom permitted to stand for more than sixty or seventy years, by which time they were of a sufficient size for the construction of timber-framed houses, or similar purposes. In this small wood - called Packway Wood - the majority of coppice stools are hornbeam, with some maple, hazel, and ash: the larger, standard trees are oak and ash.

This traditional form of management - *coppice-with-standards* - continued in some parts of East Anglia into the twentieth century. But it was in decline from the mid-nineteenth century, largely due to the increasing availability of coal following the arrival of the railways. In a few East Anglian woods the practice has been revived, usually by nature conservation groups. A coppiced wood has far more wild flowers than the densely overgrown mass of vegetation which we see here. But, overgrown though it may be, Packway Wood has at least avoided the fate of many ancient woods, which have been grubbed out for the ever-expanding arable fields, or clear-felled and replaced with monotonous conifer plantations.

As the path continues on its way we can see that Packway is one of several woods clustered in this area, and the walk here has a more pleasant, enclosed feel than it had by the airfield. The name of Heavyland Wood - which lies ahead, to the south of the path - vividly proclaims the nature of the local soils, and helps to explain why these woods are clustered here: the area was poorly drained and difficult to farm. In contrast, Abbey Wood, which lies to the north of Packway Wood, takes its name from its medieval owners, a nearby Augustinian nunnery, founded in 1258.

Arriving at the public road, the Way turns south, but shortly goes west again, along a footpath, beside yet another ancient wood, Coombes Wood. It is worth, once again, peering in through the perimeter undergrowth, for this wood has recently begun to be managed on traditional lines, and it is just possible to catch a glimpse of some recently-cut coppice stools, sprouting vigorously.

Beyond Coombes Wood, the Angles Way follows a footpath which continues through the claylands. The terrain is gently undulating, with wide arable fields. In the distance, a number of ancient farms can be seen, scattered across the countryside rather than clustered together in compact villages. Most once stood beside commons, to which their distant ancestors migrated long ago, in the early middle ages. But the commons have mostly been enclosed, usually in the early nineteenth century, so that the farmhouses now stand alone in the fields, or beside narrow lanes, with no apparent logic to their position. The path joins a lane, which it follows for a short distance, before arriving at the ploughed remains of Flixton Park.

Flixton Hall estate was owned, from the sixteenth century, by the Wyburn family, and in 1616 they began to build a new house here. This was supposedly to a design by the great architect Inigo Jones. There is a story - almost certainly apocryphal - that when Charles II asked about the house as he passed it *en route* to Yarmouth, and was told by one of his entourage that it belonged to 'a popish dog', he replied: 'Well, the dog has a beautiful kennel'. This great house was largely demolished in the 1840s, and replaced by a vast house in 'Jacobean' style, rather similar to Somerleyton, and designed by the famous Victorian architect Anthony Salvin. It was elaborate, bordering on the bizarre. With a mass of chimneys, polygonal buttresses, and pinnacles, it looked like something out of a fairy story. The estate at this time was owned by Sir Robert Shafto Adair, whose family had bought the estate in the seventeenth century. He has the distinction of having been the first, and also the last, Lord Waveney, and author of a patently crazy book about defending Britain from the menace of foreign invasion - and indigenous insurrection! This great house has itself now disappeared, demolished in 1953 after the estate was sold. Only fragments remain, converted to animal sheds. The Way passes near the estate saw mills (now converted into 'executive residences'), beside the wall of the nineteenth-century kitchen garden, and through the decaying remnants of the park, which once covered more than 200 hectares.

Much of the southern area of the park has been turned into a vast gravel pit, a sign that we have left the clay plateau, descending into the valley once more, and are on one of the great banks of glacial gravel spaced intermittently along it. Indeed, this section of the route is liberally scattered with gravel workings, a dramatic intrusion into the landscape but not an entirely new one: large-scale extraction began in the last war, to

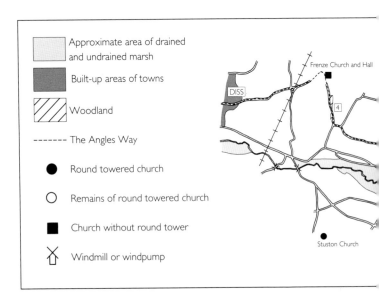

Approximate area of drained and undrained marsh

Built-up areas of towns

Woodland

------- The Angles Way

● Round towered church

○ Remains of round towered church

■ Church without round tower

Windmill or windpump

DISS

Frenze Church and Hall

4

Stuston Church

The Waveney and its valley near Homersfield.

supply the thousands of tons of gravel needed for the construction of Flixton and the other air bases nearby.

For the next few kilometres, the Way passes through the parishes of Homersfield and Mendham, along the edge of the grazing marshes. All along this stretch of the river, the rich grassland on the valley floor was reclaimed and improved many centuries ago: a task made easier by the fact that we are now beyond the reach of the tides. The boundary ditches are of various dates, the older, more sinuous ditches being of medieval origin, the straighter cuts of sixteenth-, seventeenth- or eighteenth-century date. Near Mendham, we pass back into Norfolk, and climb up onto the clayland again, but not for long. The route skirts Harleston, another fine example of a small East Anglian country town. Harleston grew up in the Middle Ages within the ancient parish of Redenhall, and with its eighteenth-century houses, its nineteenth-century Corn Exchange, and other interesting buildings it is well worth a detour. But we will resist this temptation, cross the river again by Weybread mill, and continue along the edge of the valley floor. The valley here is narrower, and the sinuous, parallel dykes suggest that the valley meadows and pastures were divided in medieval times. For six kilometres we pass through this excellent, if uneventful, landscape, before arriving at Hill Farm, and a choice. We can

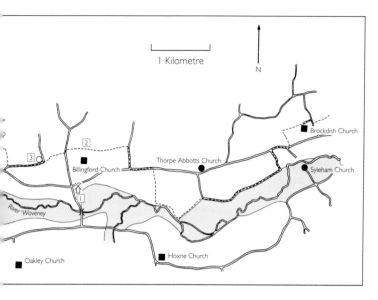

keep to the waymarked route and cross immediately into Brockdish. Or we can make a short detour, of some 200 metres, keeping to the Suffolk side of the river. This will bring us to Syleham Mill. This, with the buildings around it, may not be an especially informative or picturesque sight, but the detour is worthwhile, because it brings us into contact with an industry which was once of considerable importance all along the Waveney and Little Ouse valleys: the manufacture of linen.

This was widespread in Suffolk and Norfolk during the Middle Ages, but only as a small-scale cottage industry, producing for local consumption. In the sixteenth and seventeenth centuries, however, it became one of the most important industries in East Anglia, and one which was particularly concentrated in the valleys of the Little Ouse and Waveney. Linen cloth can be made either from hemp, or from flax. Both were grown in East Anglia, but the former was always more widely cultivated, producing as it does a more hard-wearing, durable cloth. The industry, in all its branches, was popular because it combined well with the small-scale dairy farming which flourished on the claylands in this period. It not only gave employment to linen weavers: large numbers of ancillary workers were also involved. Indeed, the labour of four or five spinners was required to keep one weaver supplied with

93

yarn, and many more were employed in the cultivation, and initial processing, of the hemp. This was a complicated business, with a number of separate stages. After being harvested, the hemp was first rotted, or *retted*, in water. Special pits were used, to avoid polluting streams, and many of the small ponds which you pass beside old farms and cottages were probably used as retting pits. Then, the hemp was dried, and crushed, using a mallet or something called a bunching block: sometimes this process was automated, and carried out by water power. Next, the central core of the plant was separated from the outer fibres. This was done by a further beating process, using an instrument called a *scutcher*. This was followed by a further beating, and then came 'heckling', or carding, when the thread was teased out ready for spinning. Only then could the thread be taken to the weaver, and used for making cloth.

In the seventeenth century, large quantities of hemp were imported from the Baltic. But even then, the majority was locally produced, and this proportion increased in the years after the Restoration. Travellers often referred to the importance of hemp growing around the Little Ouse and Waveney. Kirby, writing in the early 1730s, noted:

Syleham Mill.

> The district in which Hemp is chiefly found extends from Eye to Beccles, spreading to the breadth of about ten miles...It is in the hands of farmers and cottagers. With cottagers it is the practise to sow on the same land each year. Manuring of 16 loads of dung per acre receives great attention. Sowing is from mid to end of April, but it will bear till May. No weeding is given, for Hemp destroys every other plant.

The fields in which the crop was grown were called 'hemp-lands'. They often figure on early maps of the area. They were small, usually less than a hectare in area, and were generally located near to farms and cottages. The industry was at its peak in the 1780s. But within a few years, it declined dramatically, largely because hemp could not compete with cotton, which was said to be a quarter of the price. At the same time, there was a great increase in the price of wheat, and by 1804 Arthur Young was able to comment that 'the culture of hemp is much declined, scarcely one tenth of what it was some years past'.

By the 1840s the industry was largely dead. It hung on in

only a handful of places, including North and South Lopham, through which the Angles Way passes later, and at Diss, where one Henry Warne employed 63 people in the manufacture of *drabbets* (a material with a linen warp and a cotton weft), huckabucks, sheeting and skirting. His factory later moved to Hoxne, and lastly, to here at Syleham, which is why we have made this detour. In the mill itself - now 'Syleham House' - and in the long, low buildings behind it, on either side of the road, nearly a hundred people were employed in 1851. The buildings beside the road are still used by a clothing manufacturer, thus maintaining a thread of continuity with an ancient East Anglian industry.

Returning to the waymarked path, we cross into Norfolk again over a modern bridge, and passing through a complex of low, modern factory buildings we arrive at the village of Brockdish, partly strung out along the busy A143. It is worth pausing for a few minutes here, in spite of the traffic, to look at the houses. We have already passed a number of fine old buildings on the claylands, but this is a good place to see some of the characteristic features of the typical, 'vernacular' architecture of this part of East Anglia. The oldest houses in the village all have steeply-pitched roofs. This tells us that they were once thatched, for a thatched roof needs to be much steeper than a tiled one in order to be waterproof. They are now tiled, some with the curious, wavy 'pantiles'. These are a characteristic feature of East Anglia, although they can be found all through the eastern counties of England, and northwards into eastern Scotland. This distribution supports the suggestion that they were a Dutch invention, brought to the area in the seventeenth century, and indicative of the close contacts which East Anglia has long enjoyed with the countries on the far side of the North Sea. Not that many of the tiles were actually made in the Low Countries. They were locally produced, in rural brickyards, and were the most popular form of tile here until well into the nineteenth century.

Looking at the outside of these houses can only tell us so much. For example, it is not immediately apparent that most are timber-framed, because their exteriors are clad in later brick or coated with plaster and colour-washed. But even from the outside, it is possible to make out the distinctive plan shared by many East Anglian farmhouses built in the sixteenth and

seventeenth centuries. This is most clear in the third house you
pass on the right as you go through the village, and in the second
on the left before the Methodist church. Both have what
archaeologists like to call a *lobby-entrance* plan. The house is
only one room deep, with three main rooms on the ground floor.
Originally, these were: firstly, a 'buttery' or 'pantry' for storing
food and utensils; secondly, a 'hall', which was a kind of
general-purpose living and working room; and lastly, a 'parlour',
a more private room used by the owner and his immediate
family. The large main chimney stack is positioned along the
apex of the roof, but not centrally with the house ranged
symmetrically on either side. Instead the stack lies off-centre, in
the wall between the hall and the parlour. It usually contained
two fire places, one in the hall - which was used for cooking -
and one in the parlour. The main door to the house did not open
directly into either room, but into a small lobby backing onto the
chimney stack. From this, there was separate access to the hall
and the parlour. This arrangement provided the owner - usually a
prosperous yeoman farmer - with a measure of privacy, allowing
him to reach the parlour without having to go through the hall,
where the servants and farmhands congregated. It also provided
some protection against draughts. You can easily spot examples
of this house plan, by the way that the chimney is positioned off-
centre along the length of the building, with the main door
immediately in front of it. Many hundreds of houses of this type
were erected in the East Anglian claylands during the sixteenth
and early seventeenth centuries, when it was a prosperous
farming region, containing many moderately wealthy farmers

practising mixed dairy farming, at a time of rising population and rising agricultural prices. In later centuries, however, many were subdivided into cottages.

The Angles Way leaves the main road by the Free Methodist church, built in 1860, and climbs uphill, skirting the east and then the north of the village. Eventually it arrives at the parish church of St Peter and St Paul. The church stands, in a way that will by now be familiar, on its own, isolated within the fields. The reason, once again, is that the village migrated away from the church during the early middle ages. It is an ancient church: one of the windows in the north wall of the nave may be of pre-Conquest date, and the north windows in the chancel are certainly 'Norman' in style, and probably late twelfth-century. But the church was, like most in this part of East Anglia, altered and added to during the subsequent centuries. The aisles are early fourteenth century, the nave windows and the porch fifteenth century, and the whole building was thoroughly restored in the Victorian period, when the tower was added. It is certainly worth looking at, but perhaps of equal interest is the churchyard. This contains some of the finest eighteenth-century monuments in East Anglia, including one with beautifully carved angels, dated 1771. They must have been carved by a local mason, perhaps in Harleston or Beccles, but the stone used is limestone, brought from quarries in Northamptonshire.

A magnificent example of the stone-mason's art: late eighteenth-century headstones, Brockdish.

We are now in an area which, in terms of its landscape history, is one of the most interesting in East Anglia. Like the district around the Elmhams and Ilketshalls it displays, in the layout of its boundaries, a certain regularity, indicative of planning in the remote past. Across a wide area around Brockdish, running for many kilometres north of the Waveney, there is a marked north-south trend to the field pattern. This regularity would have been much more noticeable in the last century, before the removal of boundaries began. This semi-regular pattern is visibly disrupted by a Roman road, the 'Pye Road', the modern A140, which runs across the area at an oblique angle from north-east to south-west. In some places, the road clearly slices through individual fields and enclosures, just as a modern motorway or by-pass cuts through an earlier pattern of fields. This indicates that the regular field pattern is older than the Roman road.

Of course, not all boundaries in the area conform to the

pattern. Those in the immediate vicinity of the Roman road, for example, are laid out parallel with, or at right angles to, it. Elsewhere, boundaries and lanes on different alignments have been inserted into the older framework, often perhaps in an attempt to improve drainage, a consideration apparently of little importance to the designers of this huge grid. The latest additions to the fieldscape are the boundaries put in during the eighteenth and nineteenth centuries, when a number of open commons within the area were enclosed by Parliamentary Act. Removing all those features which we know, or reasonably

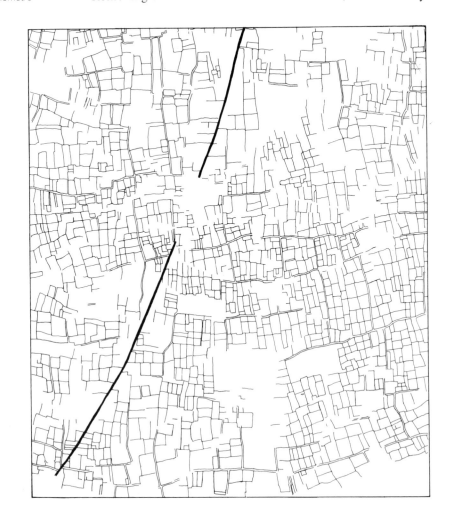

suspect, to be of Roman or later date, reveals the pattern of planning more clearly (Page 98).

How old is this vast planned landscape, and what was its purpose? The form of the field system is important here. It is not really a grid, for it has more axes which run continuously in one direction (north-south) than in the other. Archaeologists call this kind of layout *co-axial.* Examples are known from a number of areas in Britain, although they usually survive in the form of low earthworks on downland, or as tumbled walls in areas of high moorland. They range in date from the Neolithic to the Iron Age. Some are very large: on Dartmoor, in particular, there are a number of such systems, of Bronze Age date, which cover twenty or even thirty square kilometres. This Norfolk example is probably of late Iron Age origin - it may not have been very old when it was sliced by the Roman road, for it was only in the century or so before the Roman invasion that permanent settlements began to be established on the heavy boulder clays. The system must have been laid out in a landscape already largely cleared of trees: otherwise, it would have been impossible to lay out its long main axes.

We can thus be fairly sure about when this great landscape was created. But we have no idea why. One thing is certain: it does not seem to have been made for reasons connected with the practise of agriculture. Like other co-axial systems, it is - to use the archaeologists' jargon - 'terrain oblivious': its main axes run across the landscape with no regard to streams, valleys, contours. It does not seem to have been created by farmers, who would surely have sought to construct a network of ditches more responsive to the subtle contours, to help remove water from this heavy land. Instead, it has the mindless quality of an abstract design, imposed on the landscape for some other purpose. Perhaps it was created when the clays here first became permanently settled, to give each local clan or family a fair share of the new land. Perhaps it was, in some way, a symbolic creation, expressing the power and dominance of a ruler or ruling group over the landscape. We shall never know.

This striking landscape is not unique. South of Scole, the Pye Road cuts through another similar layout, centred on the village of Yaxley, and there are a number of comparable field systems running across the claylands on either side of the Waveney valley. The latter, however, are not sliced by Roman roads, and so are less easy to date. The survival of these early landscapes suggests that the area was never entirely abandoned in later centuries, in spite of the great decline in population which seems to have occurred towards the end of the Roman period. If the area had been invaded by dense woodland, then it is probable that much more of this striking layout would have been lost.

But the field system did not survive into the modern period entirely unchanged. As we have seen, boundaries were altered or new ones inserted over the centuries. During the early Middle Ages, fields were divided and divided again, through sale or inheritance, eventually leading to the fragmentation of the original units into strips, and the development of open fields. But these preserved, in the layout of their strip and furlong boundaries, the 'ghost' of the original field pattern. And this pattern was maintained when the open fields were gradually enclosed, after the Middle Ages, because this occurred in a piecemeal fashion, with individual landowners gathering together bundles of strips by purchase or exchange, and hedging them. The new fields therefore perpetuated, in a simplified form, the layout of the strips, and thus ensured the survival of substantial traces of the original, late prehistoric landscape.

The Angles Way skirts the edge of this great planned landscape for several kilometres. Leaving the church at Brockdish, it first follows lanes and, for a short distance, the busy A143, and returns to the valley. Following the edge of the meadows for a short distance, it climbs gently up the valley side once more, crosses the A143, and follows roads and tracks which are probably original features of the field system. It passes Billingford Hall - its fashionable eighteenth-century front hiding older and more rambling ranges behind - and here, on the left and largely hidden in trees, is the tiny church of St Leonard. This is another church which has been isolated through settlement migration in the early middle ages. The largest concentration of settlement in the parish lies around Billingford Common, down near the Waveney. As the path goes downhill from Billingford Hall, into a shallow dry valley, you can see, far to the left, the tower mill which stands in the middle of the common.

This is typical of many East Anglian mills, with five floors, and a distinctive, boat-shaped cap. Caps like this are sometimes said to be a 'traditional' feature of local mills, and in a sense they are, but they were actually invented in the nineteenth century, by

Englands, a firm of millwrights in Ludham in Norfolk. Billingford mill, twelve metres high and with two sets of millstones, was built in March 1860 at a cost of £1300 - a substantial sum of money at the time. It replaced a wooden post-mill which had been destroyed in the previous year. The *Norfolk News* described this event in characteristic style:

> On Thursday September 22nd during a high wind the windmill at Billingford, the property of Mr Chaplyn of Diss was blown over and in a few seconds was reduced to a heap of ruins presenting a most extraordinary spectacle. Two persons were inside the mill at the time, George Goddard the occupier and an old man in his employ. The latter was seriously hurt, insomuch as his life is despaired of, several bags of meal having alighted on his body, fracturing two or three ribs and causing other injuries. Goddard's escape was almost miraculous. He was at the top of the mill at the time of its going over...and when found was standing wedged in between the mill stones and a large cog wheel close by...Had either of these fallen upon him he must have been instantly crushed to death.

Billingford has the distinction of being both the last mill to work in Norfolk - it was still milling in 1956 - and also the first to be restored by the Norfolk Windmills Trust. It can be visited by obtaining a key from the Horseshoes Public House which stands nearby. It is some way off the route, but well worth the detour.

The path climbs up the other side of the shallow dry valley and, where it joins a track (once again, perhaps a feature of the ancient field system), the ruined round tower of Thorpe Parva church rises ahead. Thorpe was never a very large place, as its name indicates. 'Thorpe' is a Scandinavian word which simply means 'hamlet', or small settlement. 'Parva' is a Latin addition made by medieval administrators, to distinguish the parish from the nearby village of Thorpe Abbots, and means 'small'. There were only six tenants here at the time of Domesday. At the end of the seventeenth century there were a mere four dwellings, and the church was in ruins. The parish attached to the church was always tiny - no more than 140 hectares - and parishes and their churches are so concentrated in this area that it was perhaps inevitable that some should have failed. From Thorpe church back to Billingford Church is a distance of only 800 metres, and

less than a kilometre and a half to the west stands the parish church of Scole. Such a density of churches and parishes is, to a large extent, a reflection of the area's great wealth in the eleventh and twelfth centuries, when much church-building was taking place, and when parish boundaries were becoming fixed. This area may, today, be a rural backwater; but in the early Middle Ages it was flourishing, and many landowners were able to build and endow churches.

The Angles Way follows the track towards the village of Scole - and note how the field boundaries, part of the ancient field system, recede in parallel lines to the north. It then follows footpaths around the edge of Scole, before joining, for a short distance, the modern A140. As we have seen, this was, in origin, a Roman road, and a kilometre to the south of this point, where it crosses the Waveney, there was an important Roman settlement of some kind. This was perhaps just a small market town, but some people believe it was a place called *Villa Faustina*, which is mentioned in a document called the *Antonine Itinerary*, a kind of Roman route finder. If so, then it also served as a posting station, a node in the imperial communications system. Excavations here have revealed traces of substantial stone buildings of Roman date. But, as we have seen, the basic layout of the landscape around here seems to date from before the Roman period. The dominant grain of the field boundaries visible ahead, to the west as the Way leaves Scole, clearly runs at an acute angle to the line of the Roman road.

We have already mentioned that, during the early Middle Ages, the fields in this area - as in other parts of East Anglia - fragmented into strips under the impact of population growth, and were eventually organised into open fields. We are fortunate in having a very old map, probably dating to the 1580s or 90s, for part of the parish of Scole. It shows that the area through which we have just been walking was, at this date, almost entirely divided into strips. But it also shows some furlong boundaries as hard lines, and these probably represent hedges. It is probable that the landscape here - both in the sixteenth century, and earlier, in the middle ages - was never entirely hedgeless, as was the case in parts of the medieval Midlands.

Beyond Scole, the Angles Way follows a footpath, which soon becomes an overgrown sunken lane, and then a narrow path, flanked by substantial hedges. But after a while, the path becomes hedgeless, as does the landscape through which it passes. The distant view of the Waveney valley is pleasant enough, but the landscape near the path, a great sea of arable interspersed with dying oaks, left when the hedges were removed, is far from being an attractive sight. Fortunately, this rather bleak scene (enlivened only by some pylons) does not last long. We reach the road, and soon turn down a lane planted on either side with strips of woodland. These are not old, but the result of minor 'improvements' carried out in the last century by the owners of Frenze Hall. This is why they contain such ornamental species as yew, box, horse chestnut, and beech, although some older oaks - incorporated from earlier hedgerows - can be seen lurking within. As the woods come to an end, we arrive at the tiny settlement of Frenze.

This is a pleasant, rather lonely spot. Like Thorpe Parva, Frenze was always a small place. But unlike Thorpe, the church survives, though little more than a chapel opposite the manor house. It is usually locked: but, peering in at the windows, it is possible to see the seventeenth-century pulpit, and the single, apparently contemporary box-pew which it faces. Both, presumably, the gift of the Bleverhasset family, who resided in the adjacent manor house.

A little further on, we cross over a small stream by stepping-stones, and follow a track through meadows. Passing under a railway bridge, which carries the main Norwich-London line, we follow a lane lined with old hedges, full of dogwood, hazel, maple, and with an occasional hornbeam and oak. We are approaching the ancient town of Diss; but our arrival here seems to take a long time, for we have to pass first through a series of modern developments, in part a consequence of the presence of the railway station in the town. They are a reminder that the insularity, the isolation, of this part of East Anglia is beginning to break down. Almost unbelievably, some people now commute, daily, from Diss to London.

7. Commons and Riots

At last the path enters the historic core of Diss, passing the parish church of St Mary. Although extensively restored in the nineteenth century (the chancel was entirely rebuilt in 1857), this has a number of interesting features, including the arches leading through the tower at ground floor level, to allow processions to pass around the outside of the church without going out onto the street.

Diss is a good example of the kind of small market town typical of East Anglia. There was already a market here by the thirteenth century, weekly on a Friday, and larger fairs were held in July, October, and November. With the growth of the linen industry in the sixteenth and seventeenth centuries the town served as the principal local market both for hemp, and for finished cloth. Other industries have flourished here at various times, including the manufacture of corsets in the eighteenth and early nineteenth centuries and, from the turn of the present century until shortly before the Second World War, lace-making. Something of this prosperous commercial history is evident in the present appearance of the town. To the south of the church, a tapering, triangular open area stretches downhill. This is the old market place, which probably originated as a common or village green, long before the place became a market town. It was once larger, and has been partly built over in the distant past. This is clear from the layout of streets and property boundaries in the area to the west of the church, which take the form of irregular

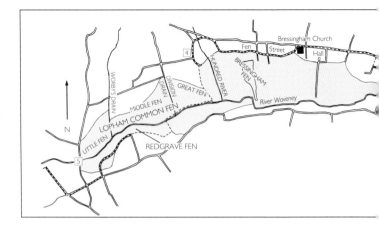

islands within a larger triangle. Such infilled market places are a characteristic feature of the topography of small market towns, in East Anglia and elsewhere. Over the years, the stalls used by medieval market traders became more substantial, and gradually they evolved into permanent shops. The buildings which now occupy these island sites are, of course, much more recent in date.

But Diss does have a number of ancient buildings, which reflect the town's prosperity in the sixteenth and seventeenth centuries. The Angles Way passes close to one, at the north-east corner of the market place, opposite the church. Formerly the Dolphin Inn, this timber-framed building, mainly of early sixteenth-century date, was originally the residence of a prosperous local merchant. The side facing towards the church is *jettied:* that is, the upper story overhangs the lower. This is a common feature of fifteenth and sixteenth-century buildings, not only in East Anglia but in many parts of England. Archaeologists and architectural historians are, as usual, divided about its origins and purpose. Some contend that it originated as a way of increasing the floor space of houses in urban areas, where ground rents were high. Others favour a structural explanation. In timber framed buildings, a large number of beams had to be jointed into the *wall plate*, that is, the horizontal beam running between the ground and upper floors. This had to hold the upright beams of the ground floor, those of the upper floor, and the floor joists. Such a proliferation of joints in close proximity would have weakened this beam, and jettying may have been

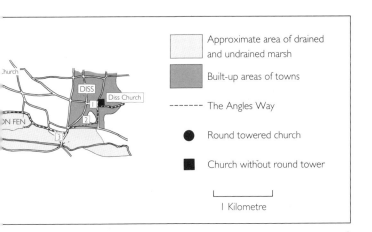

Approximate area of drained and undrained marsh

Built-up areas of towns

------- The Angles Way

● Round towered church

■ Church without round tower

|_____|
1 Kilometre

Diss Mere.

intended to avoid this by distributing these joints between two beams - the wall plate, and the beam at the front of the jetty. It is also possible that jettying helped prevent the upper floor from sagging, at a time when furniture was becoming more common

The former Dolphin Inn, Diss: a sixteenth-century timber-framed building with a projecting 'jetty'.

in houses. But whatever the reasons why jetties *began* to be built, they soon became simply a fashion. That is why, as here, they usually appear on the most important, most public facades of buildings, and are often absent from the rear.

The other houses around the market place are an interesting, visually appealing jumble, all ages and sizes. Most are fronted with eighteenth or nineteenth-century brick, but in several cases this facade conceals an older, timber-framed interior. The steep roof-lines, and the asymmetrical, often lobby-entrance plans are clear indications of this.

The waymarked path leaves the market place and turns right, skirting the edge of Diss Mere, an attractive lake covering an area of two hectares. The gardens of the houses and pubs stretch down to this, with the tower of the parish church rising above them on the right, and the grey-brick 1860 Baptist chapel in Denmark Street, with its two rather stunted west towers, to the left. The Mere, unlike the 'broads' we encountered earlier on the path, is an entirely natural feature. It was probably formed as a 'solution hollow'. Rainwater, which is slightly acid, has percolated down and dissolved an area of chalk beneath the boulder clay. The clay has slumped downwards, but still lines the hollow, allowing water to be held there. As we have seen, samples of pollen taken from sediments at the bottom of the Mere have produced much important information about the early development of the local landscape.

The Angles Way leaves the public open space around the Mere, and joins the busy A1066 for a short distance, before turning down a minor road onto Fair Green. This is an area of common land which escaped enclosure, and is surrounded by a picturesque group of houses, many of sixteenth and seventeenth-century date, including several of lobby-entrance plan. As its name suggests, Diss fair was held here during the Middle Ages. But it was also, perhaps, here that a notorious game of 'camping' took place in the middle of the eighteenth century. Camping was a traditional East Anglian sport, an early and more violent version of football, and this particular game was played by teams from Norfolk and Suffolk. Each county is said to have fielded a side of 300 men, and the game lasted fourteen hours, and resulted in the deaths of nine people. Before the match began, the Norfolk side asked their opponents whether they had brought their coffins with them. Or at least, so the story goes. The details have not been verified by modern research, and there is more than a suspicion that the story is apocryphal or, at best, grossly exaggerated. Perhaps it was disseminated in the following century, as part of a campaign to end this popular, but admittedly violent, traditional rural pastime.

The Angles Way, leaving Fair Green, follows Tottington Lane as far as the hamlet of Fen Street. Little can be seen of Roydon Fen, from which the hamlet takes its name. Its tangled undergrowth is separated from the path by the gardens and yards of the adjacent houses which have gradually encroached on it over the centuries. Roydon Fen was one of several areas of common marsh which, before enclosure in the late eighteenth and nineteenth centuries, extended in an almost continuous band along the upper reaches of the Waveney valley, and into that of the Little Ouse. They lay in shallow, saucer-like depressions which were once lakes, probably formed, as suggested in chapter one, by melting ice from the great Hunstanton ice sheet. Most have been enclosed, and at least partly drained and ploughed, but Roydon Fen has escaped more or less intact. Why the great wave of Parliamentary enclosure in the early nineteenth century, which affected most of the communities in the area, should have passed this village by is not entirely clear. It may have been that there were a large number of small proprietors here, men who had less to gain from enclosure than larger landowners, and who could - because of their numbers - block any proposals to remove the commons. Whatever the reason, the unenclosed commons in the village survived, and were the cause of serious trouble later in the century.

What precisely happened is unclear from the reports which appear in the local papers. What is undisputed is that on 7th September, 1893, the results of the election for the Board of Roydon village School were to be announced. There were a lot of people milling around the village, and these included Superintendent Tuddenham, of the Diss police, and ten of his men. He had received information that there was going to be trouble. This was connected with a bitter dispute over common rights, and over encroachments on the common made by one W.H. Hudson, in association with the Lord of the Manor, J.T. Frere - descendant of the famous archaeologist we met in chapter one. Arriving at the White Hart public house, Tuddenham found it full of men, singing, shouting and drinking. In the midst of the throng was an effigy - probably of Hudson - which some of the men were hitting. The superintendent tried to find out what was going on. The response of one of the men present, Charles Lines from Wortham, shows how misleading it is to look back to the last century as a time when law and order reigned supreme, with the police universally trusted and respected:

> Policemen get killed nowadays sometimes if they interfere too much: mind you don't.

The scene then became violent. The effigy was torn to atoms amidst uproar, and the mob advanced on Hudson's house in Snow Street. The house was stoned, and windows were smashed, as Hudson himself hid in a shed in the garden. The police intervened, and themselves came under bombardment. When Sergeant Rix was knocked unconscious by a missile, Tuddenham called out: 'You have killed this man'. Someone replied: 'We will kill you next'. The mob then proceeded to Roydon Green where they smashed up the paling which had been erected around the new enclosures, and uprooted 40 young trees which had been planted within.

Seven men were arrested, and charged with 'unlawfully and riotously assembling to disturb the public peace to the terror and alarm of her majesty's subjects'. As the accused left the court room at Diss after the initial hearing, they were wildly cheered by a large crowd waiting outside. The magistrate was greeted with hoots of derision: hardly surprising, given that he was none other than J.T. Frere, lord of the manor of Roydon!

A week later there were further disturbances, concerning a related issue. Frere was attempting to tighten up on the exercise of common rights in the parish, and had ordered his gamekeeper, Fred Culling, to exercise his rights as *Pinder* and impound any animals grazing on the common which did not legally belong there. The animals - several horses and geese - were then taken to be sold at Diss. When they arrived there, however, their owners, assisted by another large and angry mob, liberated them. The men responsible were arrested, and a separate court case commenced.

The story does not end here: the cases became famous, attracting attention from all over the country. And it is not difficult to imagine how the local people here might have resisted any erosion of their rights, for the houses and cottages of Fen Street still cluster, in a proprietorial way, around the common.

Beyond Roydon Fen, the path turns northwards onto a lane, with to the right a view of St Remigius's, the parish church of Roydon, and yet another example of a round tower (the polygonal top is a nineteenth century addition). The next section of the Angles Way is probably the least pleasant of the entire route, following as it does the busy A1066. On the left are the gardens and steam museum established by Alan Bloom. When the Way eventually leaves the busy road, however, the walker is rewarded with one of the best churches on the route, St John the Baptist at Bressingham. There was a church here in 1086, for it is mentioned in Domesday book, but nothing in the standing structure appears to be as old as this. The oldest identifiable feature is the chancel, which is probably late thirteenth century in date as it has a single surviving window in 'Early English' style. 'Early English' is the term conventionally given to the first phase of 'gothic' architecture, that is, the series of styles which feature pointed window and door openings, and which succeeded the heavier, round-arched, Norman or Romanesque style in the thirteenth century. Early English is characterised by, among other things, rather heavy and simple tracery (the intersecting ribwork in windows). It is one of the north windows of the chancel which has tracery of this simple type. Most of the visible features of the church are much later than this. The west tower was probably built in the early fifteenth century - in 1431, John Coppyng left 6/8d for the 'emdendacion' of the tower, implying that a building programme was under way at this time. The architect may have been responsible for a rather similar tower at Pulham St Mary Magdalene, fifteen kilometres north-east. The tower displays features typical of the best buildings of late medieval, 'Perpendicular' architecture in the region. The bottom of the tower, the buttresses, and the battlements all display 'flushwork', that is, the decorative use of struck flints arranged in panels defined by freestone. Most of the rest of the visible features of the church seem to be the result of a more or less sustained programme of building in the decades either side of 1500. In 1480, Alexander Hobart left money for the construction of a new north aisle, while the clerestory - that is, the line of upper windows in the nave - probably came a little later: they have an inscription which commemorates Sir Roger Pilkington, who died in 1527, and who was principal benefactor of their construction.

But there is more of interest inside. The heads of the figures on the ends of the sixteenth-century pews have almost all been broken off, and the carved faces scrubbed out. This is not mindless vandalism, but an expression of a militant ideology, of Puritan hostility towards anything smacking of idolatry. This damage was probably inflicted during the Civil War, when East Anglia was, for the most part, a staunchly Parliamentarian area. In 1644 a Captain Gilley was paid six shillings to examine the church, and to destroy 'superstitious pictures': a short time later the churchwardens' accounts record that one John Nun was paid for two days' work taking down glass and pictures, and removing inscriptions from the bells. There is much else of interest in the church, including a Jacobean pulpit, the village stocks, a horse-drawn hearse (made in 1900), and three 'collecting shoes', wooden shovels like dust-pans, dating to 1631.

Beyond the church, the Angles Way leaves the main road and once again follows a minor track, passing through another hamlet called Fen Street, with a long string of seventeenth-century cottages, some with pantiled roofs, some thatched. Here the fen, Bressingham Common Fen, disappeared through an enclosure act of 1799, which removed 464 acres of common grazing in the parish. As was usual in the Waveney valley, the open fields themselves had been enclosed piecemeal over the previous centuries: none remained to be removed by this date. Most of the fen was reclaimed, and turned into productive farmland, but the soils are so waterlogged in places that some of the allotments of land came to be used as carr woodland, and these still exist, and can be seen in the far distance, beside the river.

Beyond Fen Street we soon cross the Hundred Drain, anciently the division between Diss and Guiltcross Hundreds, and pass into the parish of South Lopham. With the adjacent parish of North Lopham, this was another major centre of the linen industry: and one which, like Syleham, continued to flourish well into the nineteenth century, with nearly a hundred looms operating in the two parishes in the middle decades of the century. Much of the hemp used was grown in the two villages. Indeed, many of the fields in the area to the north of the path were described as 'hemplands' in the Tithe Award survey of

1847. Table cloths and huckabuck towelling were still being made in North Lopham in the 1920s.

The path turns south, back towards the river Waveney, passing the edge of another small fen-edge hamlet. Here, where the waymarked path leaves the lane and passes along a track, is South Lopham Meeting House. This was built in the late eighteenth century, a small, simple structure, looking more like a house than a church. It is a reminder of the great strength of non-conformity in this part of East Anglia, from the seventeenth century onwards: something associated with the nature of the local communities, full of small freehold farmers, petty industrialists, and minor squires, rather different from the power-ful aristocratic landowners who came to dominate the communities in the areas of lighter soils further to the west.

Beyond the meeting house, to the right, a string of houses (including one thatched, seventeenth century cottage) marks the line of the old fen edge. Before the enclosure of 1815, Lopham Common Fen stretched uninterrupted from here southwards to the Waveney. Like the valley fens of the neighbouring parishes, it was used by the local communities both for grazing, and for the cutting of peat and rushes for fuel and animal bedding. Both North and South Lopham had rights to its use. At enclosure, the northern part of the Fen was allotted to the principal freeholders in the two villages, in lieu of their common rights. The allotments were first staked out on the ground and the church-wardens' accounts for North Lopham, June 6 1813, refer to the 10/- spent on 'wrighting many notices & sending em about, & many Stakes and painting em for the Fen'. But, by the usual terms of an enclosure act, they were to be 'fenced' within three calendar months, with ditches four and a half feet wide and three and a half feet deep, and with banks made with what was dug out and 'set with Thorn half hurdles or other sufficient fencing'. The

South Lopham Fen.

hedge on the left of the path is an older, pre-enclosure feature, but that on the opposite side of the field is one of those established at enclosure, although it is now somewhat gappy. This enclosed land was formed into a number of fairly small fields, and much was soon ploughed. This was possible because these fields occupied the higher, sandier ground within the fen.

The ground to the south falls gradually towards the river, and is wetter, more peaty land. Here, the land has not been drained, and Little, Middle, and Great Lopham Fens form an important nature reserve, which also includes the contiguous Redgrave Fen, in Suffolk, on the south bank of the river. This reserve, which covers an area of around 120 hectares, is partly owned and partly leased by the Suffolk Wildlife Trust. These areas have survived undrained because, at enclosure, they were not divided between the local landowners. Instead, they were allotted to the poor of Redgrave and Lopham parishes, for use as turf-cutting grounds. This in turn is probably because, given the excessively water-logged nature of the area, there was little prospect of their reclamation by local landowners at an economic cost. In the words of the Lopham Enclosure Award, the 200 acres were allotted to:

> The Lord of the Manor of Lopham, and to the Rector, Churchwardens, and overseers of the Poor...and to their respective successors for ever...For...the purpose of providing Fuel for the necessary Firing of the said poor Persons, or otherwise appropriated, and the Produce and Profits arising therefrom applied for the their use and benefit: and the Fuel so directed to be raised shall be cut, taken, and used by them, in such Quantities and Portions, and at such times in the year, and under such Orders, Rules, and Regulations, and in such manner as the Lord or Lords, Lady or Ladies of the said Manor, and the Rector, Churchwardens, and Overseers of the Poor of the said Parishes of North Lopham and South Lopham...or the major part of them, shall from time to time deem most beneficial for such Persons.

The allotted fen was to be for the use of all legally settled in the Lophams 'whether they be Owners or Occupiers' - unlike the fen before enclosure which, in theory at least, could only be used by those with defined common rights, which were attached to freehold properties. So in one sense, it could be said that the poor may have benefitted from enclosure. But on the other hand, the exploitation of the fens was no longer a *right*, to be enjoyed by poorer freeholders, but a *gift* in the hands of the local squire and richer farmers who dominated the parish. The charity accounts show that by the 1860s those responsible for administering the charity were taking money for leasing the somewhat meagre grazing in the fen, and also the shooting rights. Some of this income went to pay for the maintenance of the fences, dykes, and gates which this necessitated; the rest went to purchase bread for the poor. Ninety-two poor people in South Lopham received bread in 1873.

These valley fens may have escaped drainage, but they still bear marks of human activity in the past. Only regular grazing, or cutting for hay and reeds, keeps the marshes open. Unmanaged, large areas - especially on the margins - gradually become colonised by carr woodland, composed of alder, white willow, and ash, and, in time, by birch, oak, sycamore, and hawthorn. Decline in the use of the fen for grazing, and the dramatic fall in the rabbit population following the introduction of myxomatosis in the 1950s has accelerated this process. Like all our 'natural' environments, the valley fens are unstable, and only maintained by constant management and intervention.

Arriving at the fen, the path passes immediately through an area of alder woodland, and another, more extensive area lies beside the river. Many of the alders and some of the willows have been coppiced, some relatively recently, but most fifty years or more ago. This is clear from the way that they grow up from the ground with multiple trunks. Other areas of old coppice are evident soon after the Way crosses the river, in the north-eastern part of Redgrave Fen.

Where the fens have not been invaded by carr, they consist of open areas of grassland and reeds. The water in most of the fen percolates through the underlying chalk, and is therefore alkaline. In the western parts of Redgrave Fen, however, and in Little Lopham Fen, the water seeps in through the surrounding pockets of glacial sands and gravels, and as a result the ground water is much more acid, giving rise to an acid bog-heath. In some places, sandy soil underlies a comparatively thin layer of peat, and unusual combinations of plants occur, with alkaline-loving plants like orchids and quaking grass growing alongside heather and butterwort. Elsewhere, saw sedge and fen rush dominate the outer areas of the fen, intermixed with a wide range of species, including southern marsh orchid and marsh valerian. Near the river, and in places beside the larger drains, the vegetation is rather different because of the flow of artificial nutrients from the surrounding farmland. Here the fen is dominated by reeds, with meadow sweet, hemp agrimony, and yellow and purple loosestrife. But human activity in the past has also had its effect on the present distribution of the fen vegetation. In some of the slightly drier parts of the fen, there are extensive areas of purple moor grass. This species thrives in the calcareous soil exposed where the surface peat has been removed, long ago, by peat-cutting.

There are also some open areas of water on the reserve. As the Angles Way goes along the banks of the Waveney, it passes on the right a straight dyke. The Enclosure Award describes this as the 'Division Drain', since it was dug to separate the fuel allotment of South Lopham in Middle Fen from that of North Lopham in Great Fen, and the North Lopham churchwardens' accounts record the £10.17s.3d paid 'for Ditching the Town Land'. The water in this drain, like that in Worby's Drain, which separates Little and Middle Fen, and like that in the river Waveney itself, is somewhat sluggish. There is little fall in height across the area of the Fen. These waterways support a rather narrow range of aquatic plants, including starwort, curled pondweed, fennel-like pondweed, and floating pondweed.

There are some other old areas of open water in the Fen: small, crater-like pools. These were formed by peat-digging at various times in the past, and are famous as the only home of the Great Raft Spider, *Dolomedes plantarius*, the largest spider found in Britain (excluding the occasional oddity arriving in a crate of bananas). Most of the pools visible in the Fen have, however, been dug in quite recent times, by the Suffolk Wildlife Trust, to provide a habitat for the spiders. The original peat diggings gradually fill with silt and peat, and disappear.

The fens are a managed landscape. But they still seem like an oasis of wildness in this intensively farmed countryside. They cannot be sealed off from their surroundings, and they are affected not only by the inflow of artificial nutrients from the adjacent arable land, but also by the activities of the local water-pumping station, which (combined with the cessation of active peat cutting) has begun to cause parts of the fen to dry out.

8. The Little Ouse Valley

Somewhere around here, in the tangled undergrowth on the western side of Little Fen, lies the source of the river Waveney. A few hundred metres further west, the Little Ouse begins. The valley, however, continues without a break, and with little change in the scenery. Passing through the end of yet another hamlet called Fen Street, the Way proceeds through the northern part of Redgrave parish and arrives at another important area of undrained fen, Blo Norton and Thelnetham Fens. These have a similar history to the Lopham and Redgrave Fens, being the remnants of much wider areas of fen which have survived because, being the most poorly-drained parts, they were allotted to the poor for fuel when enclosure took place. The common fen at Blo Norton was enclosed in 1822; that at Thelnetham in 1818. Yet although allotted as turbaries, turf cutting probably did not continue on a large scale for very long after enclosure. In Blo Norton, in 1875, the Charity Commissioners agreed to reorganise the charity. As a result,

> The Trustees shall take steps to discontinue the gratuitous use of any portion of the land...for the purpose of cutting and getting fuel therefrom.

Having lost their common rights over the Fen, the community now lost any right to cut peat. Instead, the income from leasing the Fen was to be used to purchase coal, or other

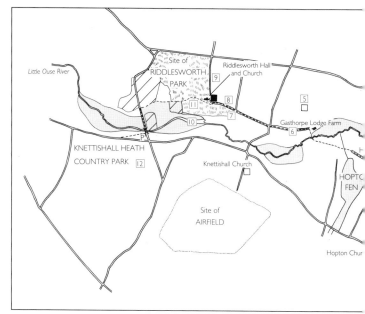

fuel, which was to be sold 'at a reduced cost to deserving poor persons'. The trustees could also use the money for a number of other charitable purposes, including special payments to 'deserving and necessitous persons'.

Once again, the plant communities within the Fen are varied. In places least affected by drainage, there is a great range of calcareous fen vegetation, including saw sedge but also black bog rush, fen orchid, long-stalked yellow sedge, quaking grass, as well as a small colony of grass of parnassus. Elsewhere, where there is some drying out in the summer, this range of plants is replaced by taller vegetation dominated by reed, and meadow sweet, with hemp agrimony and purple loosestrife. As in Redgrave and Lopham Fens, patches of purple moor grass mark where the turf has been stripped in the past by the local people. And here, too, the edges of the fens have been invaded by carr woodland, with - on the drier parts of Blo Norton Fen - some ash and oak. Some of this woodland has been coppiced in the past and the path goes past stools of alder, birch, and some sallow willow.

As the path leaves the fen, the black tower of Thelnetham mill rises above the fields to the right. What could be a more

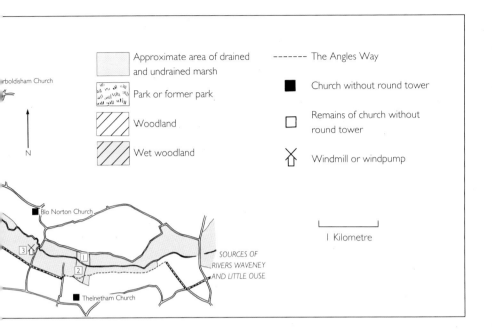

Legend:
- Approximate area of drained and undrained marsh
- Park or former park
- Woodland
- Wet woodland
- ------- The Angles Way
- ■ Church without round tower
- □ Remains of church without round tower
- Windmill or windpump

N

rboldisham Church

Blo Norton Church

3

SOURCES OF RIVERS WAVENEY AND LITTLE OUSE

2

Thelnetham Church

1 Kilometre

typically East Anglian sight? Visiting the mill involves a slight detour, of about 200 metres. But it is a detour impossible to resist. The mill was built in 1819 for one Mr William Buttons, probably by the millwright George Blomefield, who lived in the village and who built several other windmills in the area. It was erected before the enclosure of Thelnetham Fen in 1821, and thus originally stood in an area of open common land - just as Billingford mill still does. We know from the diary of a local carpenter, Thomas King, that it was erected and fitted out with remarkable speed. Construction began in July 1819, and on Christmas Day of the same year it began to grind corn. It continued to do so for more than a century, finally ceasing, in a damaged and deteriorated state, in 1926. After a long period of dereliction the mill was sold in 1979 to the Suffolk Mills Group, who began restoration work. It is now in working order, and is generally open to the public at weekends during the summer. It provides a good idea of the way East Anglian mills looked and worked before their decline in the early years of this century.

But something needs to be said about windmills in general, in order to understand this particular example. The earliest type of windmill known in East Anglia, and indeed in England as a whole, was the *post mill*, introduced into this country during the twelfth century. In these structures the entire body of the mill - containing stones and machinery - stands on a massive central post, on which it can be rotated in order to bring the sails into the wind. The earliest surviving post mills date from the seventeenth century, although there are none as old as this in Norfolk or Suffolk. A late eighteenth-century example - although now without its sails - stands at Garboldisham, two kilometres to the north-west of Thelnetham mill, within 500 metres of the line

Thelnetham Mill.

of the Angles Way. Another, recently restored, can be found at Stanton, eight kilometres south of Riddlesworth. Such mills continued to be built into the nineteenth century, but they were gradually superseded by the more efficient *tower mill.* In this, the stones and other machinery were mounted in a brick or stone tower, which was surmounted by a moveable cap in which the *windshaft,* or main axle, and the sails, were mounted. Only the cap had to be turned into the wind, although in the earliest mills this still had to be done manually, by means of a long pole hanging down from the back of the cap. Moreover, the sails were the same as those which had been used on all windmills since the middle ages: that is, they were 'common' sails, simple wooden frames on which canvas was spread. The miller had to continually stop the mill and adjust the canvas, whenever there was a marked change in wind speed. Minor gusts could not really be catered for at all.

We often think of windmills as rather archaic machines, superseded by the new technologies of the Industrial Revolution. But windmills did not rapidly fall out of favour in the late eighteenth century, and the spirit of technological innovation which characterised this period did not pass them by. It was in the corn growing areas of eastern England, and particularly in East Anglia, that the innovations were most widely adopted. The first of these came in 1745, when Edmund Lee invented the 'fantail', or 'fly'. This was a small vaned wooden wheel attached to the back of the cap, at right-angles to the sails, and connected through gears to a winding mechanism. As the wind changed direction, the fantail rotated and turned the cap of the mill, so that the sails always faced into the wind. No longer did the miller have to haul the cap into the wind by means of a long tail pole, and the mill could respond, almost instantaneously, to quite minor fluctuations in wind direction.

Next, in 1772, came the invention by the Scottish millwright Andrew Meikle of a totally new kind of sail. This was composed of a large number of parallel shutters, arranged widthways across the sail and connected by a long rod or 'shutter bar'. A spring at the windshaft end kept the shutters closed under normal conditions, but allowed them to open during gusts. This improvement was followed in 1807 by a further refinement, made by the Norfolk millwright and engineer William Cubitt, who was the engineer responsible for the construction of the

New Cut on the Lowestoft-Norwich navigation. This was the *Patent Sail*, in which the opening of the shutters was controlled by a rod, connected to a complicated mechanism called a 'spider' at the point where the sails joined the windshaft. The windshaft itself was hollow - cast now in iron, rather than made of wood - and a rod ran from the spider, through the windshaft, to a rack-and-pinion drive. This was controlled by a chain which hung down the back of the mill. By moving this, the rod controlling the shutters could be moved up or down, and thus the shutters themselves could be opened or closed. Weights could be hung on this chain, so that the shutters could be kept closed against wind pressure, but allowed to open if there were gusts. Changing the weights could therefore allow for changes in wind conditions without stopping the mill. The result of these eighteenth and nineteenth-century innovations was that the windmill became, for the first time, a controllable and comparatively sophisticated machine, rather different from the simple structure of earlier centuries.

When originally built, Thelnetham mill must have struck the local inhabitants as new and innovative. Although tower mills had appeared in other parts of East Anglia during the eighteenth century, Thelnetham was probably the first to be erected in the immediate area. Nevertheless, it was really rather an old-fashioned structure. It does not seem to have had a fantail, and was equipped with the old 'common' sails. Why this should have been so is not entirely clear. It may have been that the millwright was unfamiliar with the latest developments in mill technology. Or perhaps Mr Buttons lacked sufficient resources to pay for the best milling equipment. Whatever the reason, things changed radically a few years later. The carpenter Thomas King notes, in an entry in his diary, 'Mr Wm Buttons cast iron shaft put up July 16th 1832', and this replacement of the original shaft was almost certainly made in order to fit the Cubitt's patent sails which now grace the mill. This second shaft is still in use, and bears the raised inscription 'J.AICKMAN.LYNN.1832': Aickman, who had established his foundry in 1827, was a major supplier of windmill shafts in Cambridgeshire and Suffolk. The fantail, and the iron rack to the kerb, were probably added at the same time. A little belatedly, Thelnetham mill had become a modern machine.

As with water mills, the centralised milling of flour at the

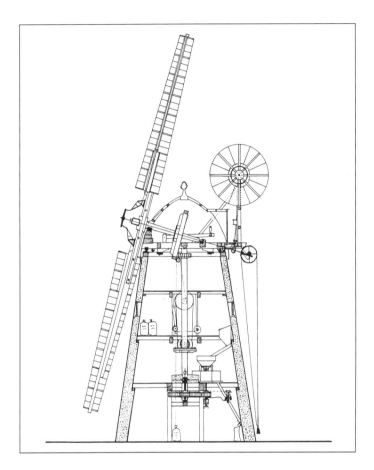

Diagram showing the
internal workings of
Thelnetham Mill.

major ports deprived windmills of their original purpose. But
Thelnetham mill, like many others, kept going for a while by
milling animal feed. Now restored, it is a fine sight, with its
black tower - tarred to make the interior waterproof - and its
gaily coloured fan-tail painted in red, white and blue stripes - in
honour of Queen Victoria's jubilee!

Beyond the mill, the path continues beside the flood-plain of
the Little Ouse. This was occupied by areas of common pasture
and fen before they were enclosed at various dates in the early
nineteenth century. Their names live on, spread across the face
of the Ordnance Survey map: Raydon Common, Garboldisham
Common, Hopton Common. Much of the valley floor in this
stretch is now under the plough.

Since we left Beccles, we have been surrounded on all sides by the boulder clay plateau. But now the clay comes to an end, and we enter a very different landscape, that of the Breckland. We have already mentioned this strange, sandy area, and discussed how after the Middle Ages it suffered much depopulation; how it was an area of extensive warrens and heaths; how in the eighteenth and nineteenth centuries it saw the spread of great estates, large houses and parks; and how, in the years after 1920, much of the area was transformed by the activities of the Forestry Commission. These key themes in the history of the Breckland landscape are well illustrated by features which we shall encounter on this final stage of the Angles Way.

The first clues that we have reached the edge of the Breckland come soon after the path leaves the former area of Hopton common. The path recrosses the river and ahead the ruined tower of Gasthorpe church can be seen, isolated on the hill above the valley. As with other examples of isolated churches, St Nicholas stands alone because the community which it served migrated to the edges of neighbouring commons during the early middle ages. In this case the settlement moved to the great areas of common grazing in the floor of the valley of the Little Ouse. But the church is ruined because, with depopulation and economic decline on these difficult soils during the fifteenth and sixteenth centuries, the community could no longer afford its upkeep. The same story, with the same results, can be found again and again in and around the Breckland. Indeed, only a few hundred metres down the path, another example can be glimpsed, on the far side of the valley. Now, however, the ruined Knettishall church is experiencing a rather curious new lease of life through conversion into a modern 'executive' dwelling!

The village of Gasthorpe has not suffered the fate of some in the Breckland, which have disappeared completely. But it has dwindled. After migration from the church to the common, it probably took the form of a straggling line of farms and cottages, along the edge of the valley bottom fen. With population decline, this row has become gappy and disconnected, with Gasthorpe Lodge Farm quite isolated from the main concentration of settlement. Discoloured soil in the ploughed fields, and low bumps or earthworks in the pastures near the farm, strongly suggest that the area in between was once occupied by other dwellings.

The surviving portion of Gasthorpe village stands on what is probably a minor north-south Roman road. It is a picturesque enough place, especially the thatched old post office, and the sixteenth- or early seventeenth-century house with a jetty, which stands to the south of the path. But there is something not quite right about this group of cottages. They look too good, too picturesque. It may be that their appearance owes something to the proximity of the Riddlesworth estate. The nineteenth-century owners may have altered the appearance of an existing settlement to fit in with the prevailing taste for the picturesque which we met earlier at Somerleyton.

The village of Riddlesworth, like Gasthorpe and Knettishall, declined in prosperity and population in the fifteenth and sixteenth centuries, and more and more of its land was gathered into the hands of its manorial lords. In the sixteenth and seventeenth centuries, Riddlesworth was the seat of the Drury family, including Drue Drury, one of the gaolers of Mary, Queen of Scots. A descendant of the Drurys, Sir William Wake, sold the estate to Sylvanus Bevan in about 1785. Bevan was a man with ideas, and under him the appearance of the landscape around Riddlesworth and Gasthorpe was transformed. He demolished the old Elizabethan manor house, and constructed a new hall a little to the south. This was a large classical house, with Venetian windows set in blank arches, two storeys high above a rusticated basement. It was built of pale yellow brick with stone dressings.

The new hall was only one part of an extensive building programme, which included new farmhouses, farm buildings, and estate cottages. The total bill for all this was more than £7,000, no mean sum in the late eighteenth century. Yet this was only part of a wider scheme of landscape improvement. Under Bevan's direction, open fields, heaths, warrens and sheep-walks, in Riddlesworth and the surrounding parishes, were enclosed into large rectangular fields. These were surrounded by neat hawthorn hedges in which Bevan also planted crab apple and sweet briar. The fields were systematically 'clayed', that is, the sandy soil was mixed with chalky clay dug from nearby pits, in order to improve its consistency and fertility. In addition, meadows in the valley of the Little Ouse were 'floated', or irrigated, to encourage an early crop of grass. But above all,

Riddlesworth: the late
eighteenth-century
hall built by Sylvanus
Bevan, which was
burnt down in 1899.

Bevan embarked on a massive campaign of tree-planting, planting over a million trees in the park and surrounding landscape. In all this, of course, Bevan was not unique. This was the great age of agricultural improvement in Norfolk, and other landowners in this period were similarly concerned with improving the farming, and the appearance of the landscape, on their estates.

Sylvanus Bevan sold the Riddlesworth estate in the early nineteenth century to Thomas Thornhill, whose family in turn sold it, in 1893, to Mr W.N. Champion, of Cantley Hall near Doncaster in Yorkshire. By this time, the estate extended over more than 1,700 hectares, in an area which was now (as a result of the late nineteenth-century agricultural depression) principally famed for its game. The *Norfolk Chronicle* for 23 September 1843 described it as 'One of the finest sporting and residential estates in the County'. It was a snip at 'a price that does not fall far short of £60,000'. In 1899 the hall burnt down, and was replaced by the vast new building which stands here today. The Champion's descendant, a Mrs Noel, sold the hall to Riddlesworth School, which now owns and occupies the premises.

A minor, and slightly bizarre, sign of the estate's impact on the landscape can be found a few hundred metres after leaving Gasthorpe. Large quantities of lilac appear in the hedge beside the path, presumably planted in order to 'improve' the appearance of the drive some time in the nineteenth century. A little further on the track arrives at the old lodge house. The building is unmistakable, constructed as it is of the same pale yellow brick, and with the same blank recessed arches, as the Riddlesworth Hall built by Bevan in the late eighteenth century. Its simple, rather austere classical lines were subsequently altered by the insertion of appropriately picturesque, pointed, gothic windows! This may have been done towards the end of the nineteenth century, when the building was used as a school. A more striking example of 'picturesque' landscaping occurs to the right of the path, a little further along, in the form of a symmetrical nineteenth-century estate cottage, with thatch and decorative barge-boards. Such features would once have acted as signals that the centre of the estate was being approached. Sure enough, a little further on, the track arrives at Riddlesworth Hall, with the parish church standing beside it.

Just before the church, looking to the right, you can see in the far distance the kitchen garden, which was built by Bevan at the end of the eighteenth century. As is often the case, it lies at some distance from the hall. As we saw at Somerleyton, the fashion then was for the house to stand in isolation, with the open grass of the parkland running right up to its walls. Walled kitchen gardens were, in this context, considered an unsightly intrusion. But this did not mean that their owners avoided all contact with them. Against the south wall of the kitchen garden at Riddlesworth, and just visible from the path, is an early nineteenth-century summer house. It is an impressive building, with a hipped slate roof, an open south facade of wooden Ionic pillars, and a carved frieze. The walled garden, while unacceptable within the park, still had its own particular appeal, as a place to sit, and perhaps picnic, in fine weather.

The parish church of St Peter now serves not only Riddlesworth but also the adjacent parish of Gasthorpe. Its survival probably owes more to its proximity to a country house than it does to the size of the local community, for Riddlesworth village is virtually non-existent, consisting of the hall, and a few outlying estate farms and cottages. The contrast between its survival, and the failure of the churches at Gasthorpe and Knettishall, is neatly reflected in the presence within it of a fine Jacobean pulpit brought from Knettishall. The church has been heavily restored by successive owners of the hall, some of whom are buried within it. The most important monument is that to Sir Drue Drury, who died in 1617.

After leaving the church the path passes through a small area of ornamental woodland, probably planted in the early nineteenth century and much decayed, although now being replanted. Like many such woods, it was under-planted with box and yew, examples of which still survive beside the path. The Way then crosses an open lawn, providing a fine view of the Hall, built by the Champions after the destruction of the old hall 1899. Designed by the Norwich architect H.J. Green, it was begun in 1900. It is an impressive building, and a slightly unusual one, in that it is classical in style, arranged around a pediment of Corinthian columns, yet asymmetrical in its layout. It is also unusual in that it was built at a time when relatively few country houses of any size were being erected in East Anglia. In this period the fortunes of the great landed estates were declining, largely because agriculture was in a state of recession after the 1870s. As farmers suffered, rents from agricultural land declined. Those who, like the Champions, could afford to build houses on this scale were often new families, not local to the area, who had made their money in finance, trade, or industry.

Beyond the hall, the path runs through what was once Riddlesworth park. This is now almost entirely under the plough, except for a small area near the hall, which the school uses as playing fields. Nevertheless, a number of parkland features survive, and can be seen from the path. The park was created by Sylvanus Bevan in the 1790s, following the closure of a number of public roads running through the area to the north of the house. The earlier Elizabethan hall had stood beside a public

Riddlesworth Hall.

road, with only a relatively small area of gardens around it. The huge cedar of Lebanon standing to the north of the hall, which is clearly visible from the path, was (to judge from its size) originally planted in these gardens. Bevan's park covered around 120 hectares, and contained a number of circular clumps and plantations, as well as many single trees. In the south of the park the Little Ouse was widened to form a thin lake. There was a small central island, on the northern shore of which a boat house stood. This lake survived well into the twentieth century, but has now entirely disappeared.

Writing in 1840, James Grigor, a Norwich nurseryman and author of a book on Norfolk's trees entitled *The Eastern Arboretum*, was complimentary about what must still have appeared a rather young landscape.

> Riddlesworth hall is pleasantly situated in an extensive park, which is beautifully varied with vegetation. Its chief trees are of oak, elm, and cedar; one of the last stands in front of the hall and is of handsome character.

The park changed little during the nineteenth and twentieth centuries. Unlike many members of the landed gentry, who seem to have changed the details of their parks and gardens every five minutes, successive owners of Riddlesworth were largely content to leave the landscape as it was. Some slight changes were made to the outline of the clumps and plantations, and a minor expansion of the park occurred towards the south east, but the 1892 Ordnance Survey six-inch-to-the-mile map of Riddlesworth shows the park much as it had been a hundred years before.

The path, after leaving the hall, skirts the edge of Ladies Grove, one of Bevan's larger clumps, planted with oak, horse chestnut, but mainly beech. The size of the beech trees indicates that they are relics of the original planting. The remains of other clumps and belts can be seen in the distance to the north, and, some 500 metres further on, there is another large wood planted by Bevan. This again consists of old beech, although this time underplanted with spindle and blackthorn. Finally, where the track meets the public road, there is another lodge, again of grey-yellow brick and with recessed arches (the recessed arch here is largely obscured by a later extension).

The path turns south, following the public road. Even here

we have not quite escaped from signs of the estate - the bridge by which the road crosses the river, and over which we return once more to Suffolk, was constructed by the estate as part of the improvements carried out in the nineteenth century.

Estates like Riddlesworth were partly responsible for the enclosure and destruction of the heaths which, before the nineteenth century, occupied so much of the Breckland. Most of the surviving fragments disappeared under the great conifer plantations which, under the management of the Forestry Commission, spread inexorably across the area during the 1920s and 30s. But some survived, either because they were never formally enclosed or because, although enclosed, they were never brought into cultivation, planted with trees, or otherwise 'improved'. The largest area of open heathland in Breckland lies some fifteen kilometres north-west of the line of the Angles Way, and owes its current survival to its use by the army as a Battle Training Area. But there are a number of smaller pockets, many of which are protected as nature reserves, or as Sites of Special Scientific Interest. The Angles Way terminates at one of these - Knettishall Heath. This area of 150 hectares is now a Country Park, managed by Suffolk County Council which leases the land from the owners, the Riddlesworth estate. The Heath is crossed by an important Roman Road, the Peddars Way, which is now a long distance footpath running north to the coast. This connects with the North Norfolk Coastal Path which, in turn, joins the Weavers' Way, which runs to Yarmouth - where the Angles Way begins!

As we described earlier, the open heathland landscape of the Breckland was first created in the Neolithic and Bronze ages, and a kilometre away across the heath from the end of the Angles Way there is a Bronze Age round barrow, probably constructed around 2000 BC. It is not a massive feature - around two metres high, and 30 metres in diameter - but, dramatically crowned by a Scots pine tree, and in a remote and often lonely location, it is nevertheless an imposing sight. Built, in all probability, on open pasture beyond the margins of the arable land, it owes its subsequent survival to the fact that the land on which it stands has never been ploughed. Throughout the Roman period, and into the middle ages, these dry soils were grazed by sheep. Rabbits, too, later became important here, and archaeological evidence for this can be found on the heath, in the

form of a wide, low circular mound, surrounded by a ditch and low outer bank. This is almost certainly a seventeenth or eighteenth-century enclosure for keeping breeding does and their young safe from predators and poachers, before being released onto the open heath. Originally, the low outer bank would have taken the form of a turf wall, topped with gorse, which would have made a very effective barrier against rabbits - as long as it was regularly maintained.

But the heath, a relatively constant and unchanging landscape for at least three thousand years, has altered dramatically this century. Because sheep grazing declined, and because rabbit

Aerial view of Knettishall Heath. Much of the heath has been invaded by scrub woodland since the early years of this century. Systematic attempts are now being made to reverse this process.

View on Knettishall Heath.

numbers fell in the 1950s and 1960s as a result of myxomatosis, it began to be invaded by scrub which, in time, developed into woodland, composed mainly of birch and oak, but with some Scots pines. This has happened with remarkable speed. Aerial photographs taken by the RAF in 1946 show that only some 20% of the heath was covered with trees. By the 1980s, this figure had risen to nearly 50%, with the result that over wide areas the traditional heathland vegetation had been obliterated. This is, of course, yet another example of how even our most 'natural' landscapes are the result of human intervention, and of traditional management practices. The County Council is now attempting to reduce the number of trees on the heath, so that the open areas are increasing in extent once again. These areas are quite stunning. Over most of the heath, the soils are very acid, and the heathland vegetation is dominated by a mixture of heather, bracken, and a variety of sedges and grasses, with extensive stands of willow herb. There are numerous other flowering plants, most noticeably harebell and heath bedstraw. It is a beautiful and fascinating area, and one which emphasises once again a recurrent theme of the entire route: how much the landscape owes to the influence of man. A survivor from one of the most distinctive of East Anglia's traditional landscapes, it is a fitting end to the Angles way.

Index

Numbers in brackets indicate illustrations.

Villa Faustina 103
Wainford 77-81, (77), (80)
Wangford Hundred 73
Warne, Henry 95
Warrens 22, 23, 124
Washlands 27
Water Mills 81, 84
Wentworths 44
West Stow 21
Wherries 36, 52, 80-1, (52), (80)
Wicker Well 44
Windmills 13, 100-1, 118-23, (120), (123)
Wind Pumps 13, 27, 28, 67, 68, (29)
Woodland, ancient 89-90
Woodland, carr 62, 63, 64, 112, 115, 118
Woolsey Mill 28
Worlingham 66-8
Worlingham Wall 60, 61, 66, (60)
Yare, river 17, 25, 36, 57, 58
Yarmouth, Great 10, 13, 16, 25, 26, 28, 36, 55,
59, 64, 75, 76
Yaxley 99